柔術

Jujutsu 1913

虎之巻

The Tiger Scroll

By Noguchi Senryuken 野口潜龍軒

Translated by Eric Shahan ジャパン・エリッツ

虎之卷　會員專用　禁讓與賃借

非賣品

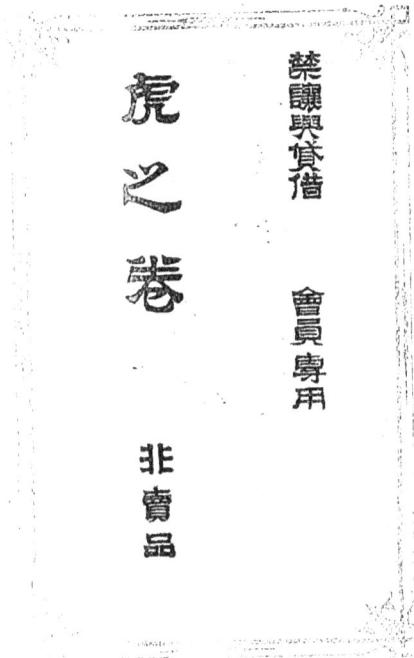

Tora No Maki
The Tiger Scroll
Transferring or Lending Forbidden
For the use of members only
Not For Sale

Translator's Introduction:

The author Noguchi Senryuken and his brother Masahachiro founded a jujutsu school that offered both in-person training at their Tokyo dojo as well as mail-order training so groups and individuals could train independently. These remote students would use Noguchis' series of instructional books as training guides. These books were republished and re-packaged over several years, with many books having the same title but modified contents.

The subtitle of this book, *The Tiger Scroll,* has a companion volume subtitled *The Dragon Scroll,* which contains detailed instructions on how to perform each of the techniques described in *The Tiger Scroll.* I am planning to translate all the books in this series.

奥秘

柔術教授書

巻之虎

帝國尚武會藏版

野口潜龍軒監修

帝國尚武會編纂

Inner Secrets : A Jujutsu Instructor's Manual
The Tiger Scroll
Director : Noguchi Senryuken
Imperial Martial Enlightening Guild

本 部 事 務 所 と 野 口 會 長

Chairman Noguchi and the Honbu, Head Office.

本部道場と野口範師長

Noguchi Shihan, Head Instructor, and the Honbu Dojo.

第一圖

鉛垂線と基底

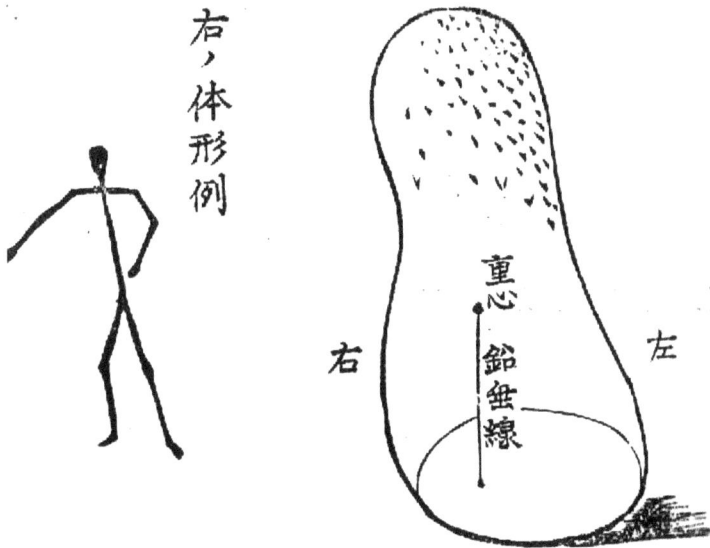

右ノ体形例

重心

鉛垂線

右　　　左

第二圖

力點支點及重點

右ノ体形例

力点

支点

重点

Illustration 1
Plumb Line and the Base

How the body is positioned according to the diagram on the right.

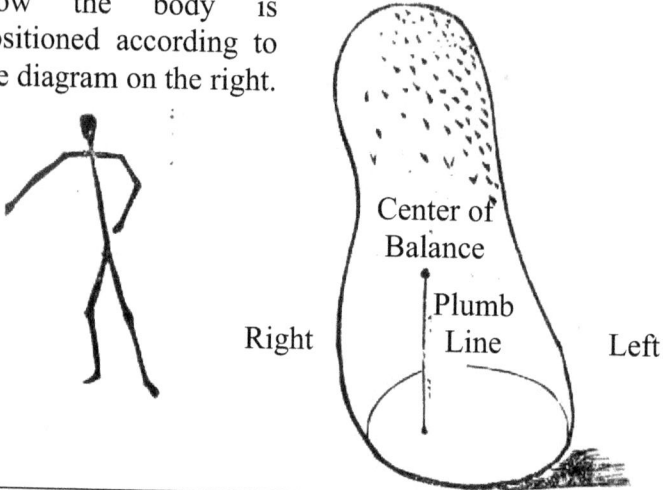

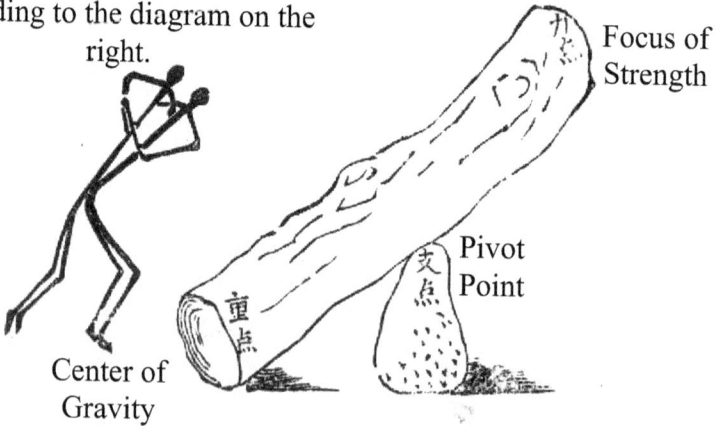

Center of Balance

Plumb Line

Right

Left

Illustration 2
Focus of Strength, Pivot Point & Center of Gravity

How the body is positioned according to the diagram on the right.

Focus of Strength

Pivot Point

Center of Gravity

第　三　圖

丹田集力法の體勢

Illustration 3

Posture for focusing your power in Tanden.

法　別　上　同

Illustration 3.1

Another posture for focusing your power in Tanden.

圖 四 第

勢 體 の 法 力 集 拳 握

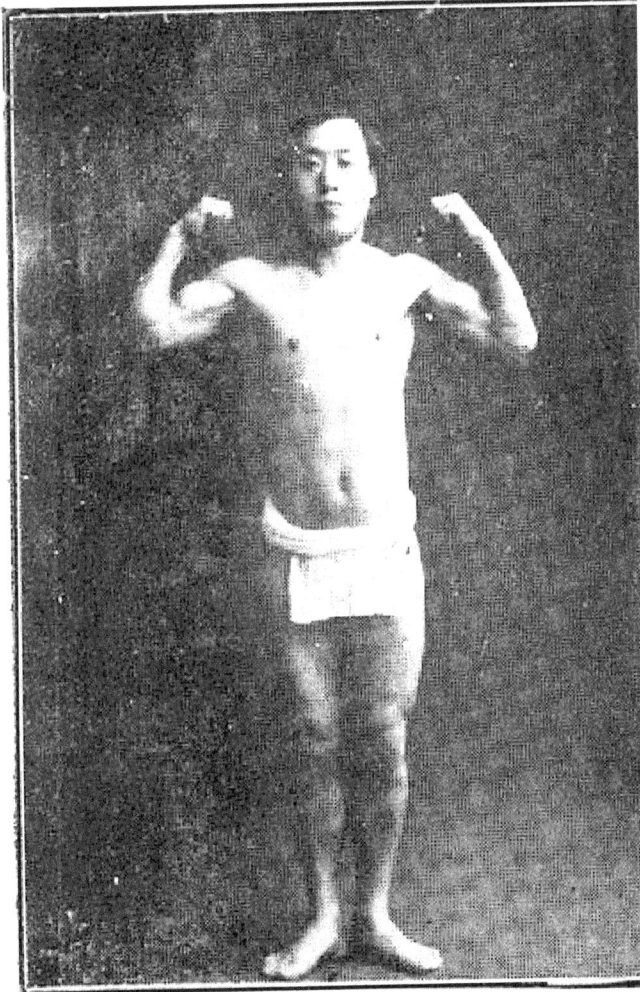

Illustration 4

Posture for focusing power in your grip.

第五式圖
舊式稽古着

襦袢

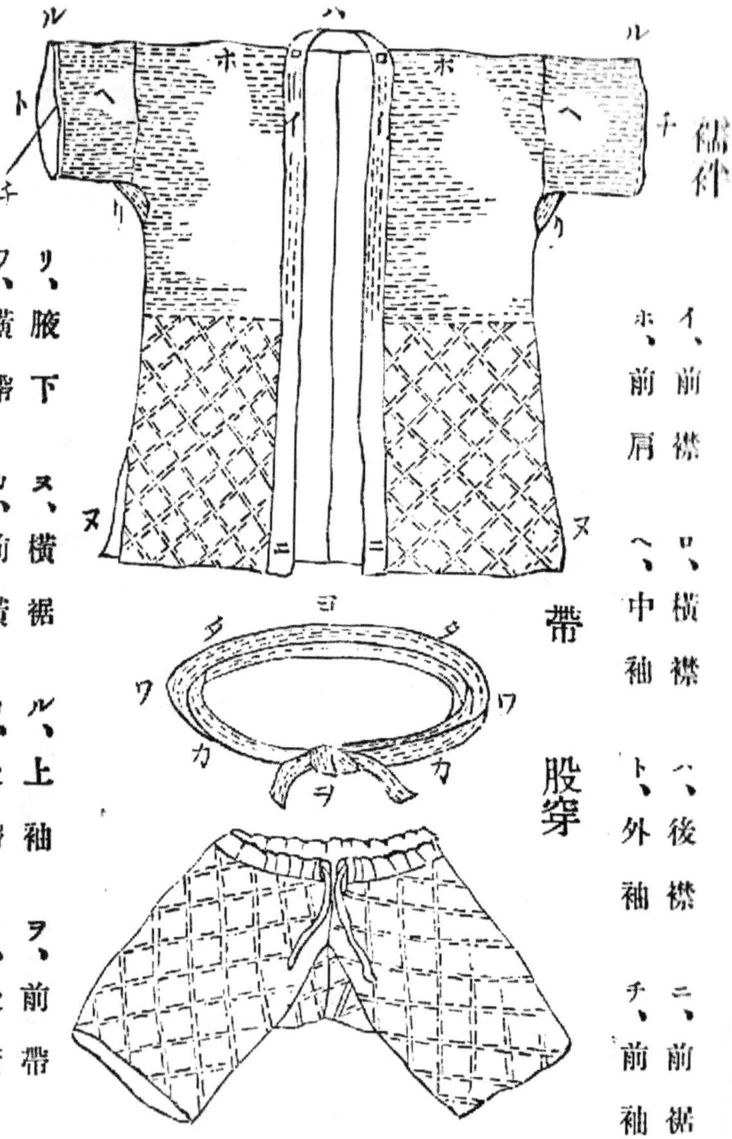

イ、前襟
ロ、横襟
ハ、後襟
ニ、前裾
ホ、前肩
ヘ、中袖
ト、外袖
チ、前袖

帶
股穿

リ、腋下
ヌ、横裾
ル、上袖
ヲ、前帶
ワ、横帶
カ、前横
ヨ、後帶
タ、後横

12

Illustration 5
Old Style Keikogi Training Uniform

ワ、横帯	Side of the Obi (Belt)	リ、腋下	Under Armpit	ホ、前肩	Front of Shoulder	イ、前襟	Front of the Collar
カ、前横	Front Side	ヌ、横裾	Side Hem	ヘ、中袖	Middle of Sleeve	ロ、横襟	Side of the Collar
ヨ、後帯	Back of Obi	ル、上袖	Upper Hem	ト、外袖	Outside of Sleeve	ハ、後襟	Back of the Collar
タ、後横	Back Side	ヲ、前帯	Front of Obi	チ、前袖	Front of Sleeve	ニ、前裾	Front of Hem

Obi Belt	Matahaki Shorts	Juban Top

13

新式稽古着

濡袢の背面

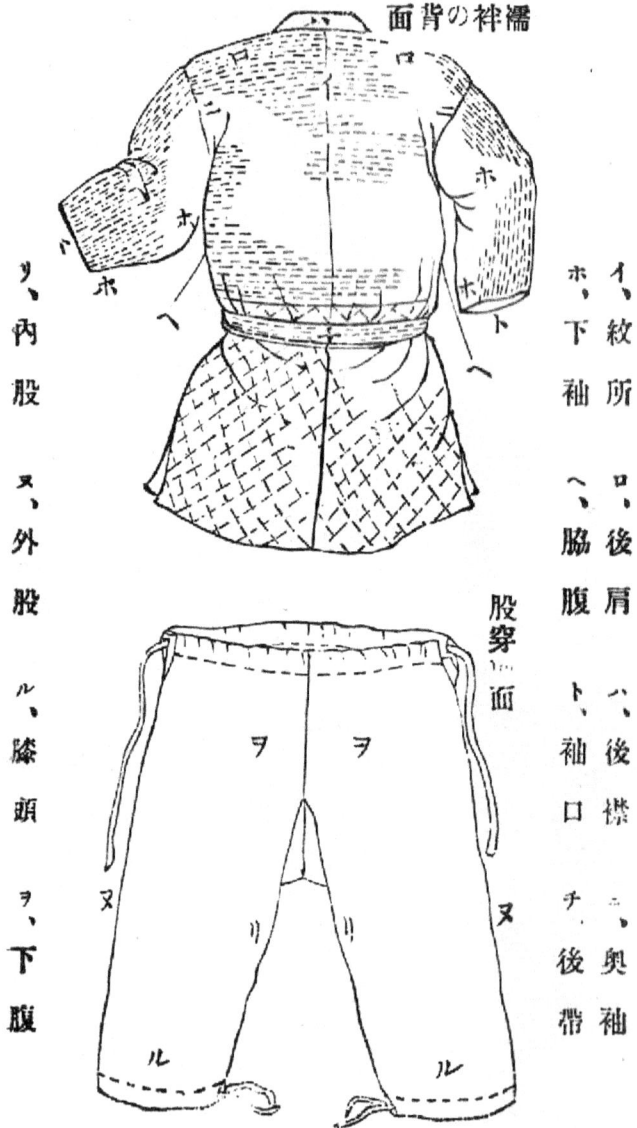

イ、紋所　ロ、後肩　ハ、後襟　ニ、奥袖
ホ、下袖　ヘ、脇腹　ト、袖口　チ、後帯

股穿面

ヲ、内股　ヌ、外股　ル、膝頭　ヲ、下腹

リ、内股　ヌ、外股　ル、膝頭　ヲ、下腹

14

Illustration 6
New Style Keikogi Training Uniform

リ、内股	Uchi-mata	ホ、下袖	Lower Sleeve	イ、紋所	Place where family crest goes
ヌ、外股	Soto-mata	ヘ、脇腹	Side of Abdomen	ロ、後肩	Back of Shoulder
ル、膝頭	Top of Knee	ト、袖口	Sleeve Opening	ハ、後襟	Back of Collar
ヲ、下腹	Bottom of Abdomen	チ、後帯	Back of Obi	ニ、奥袖	Sleeve Meets Shoulder

第 七 圖

人 體 方 位

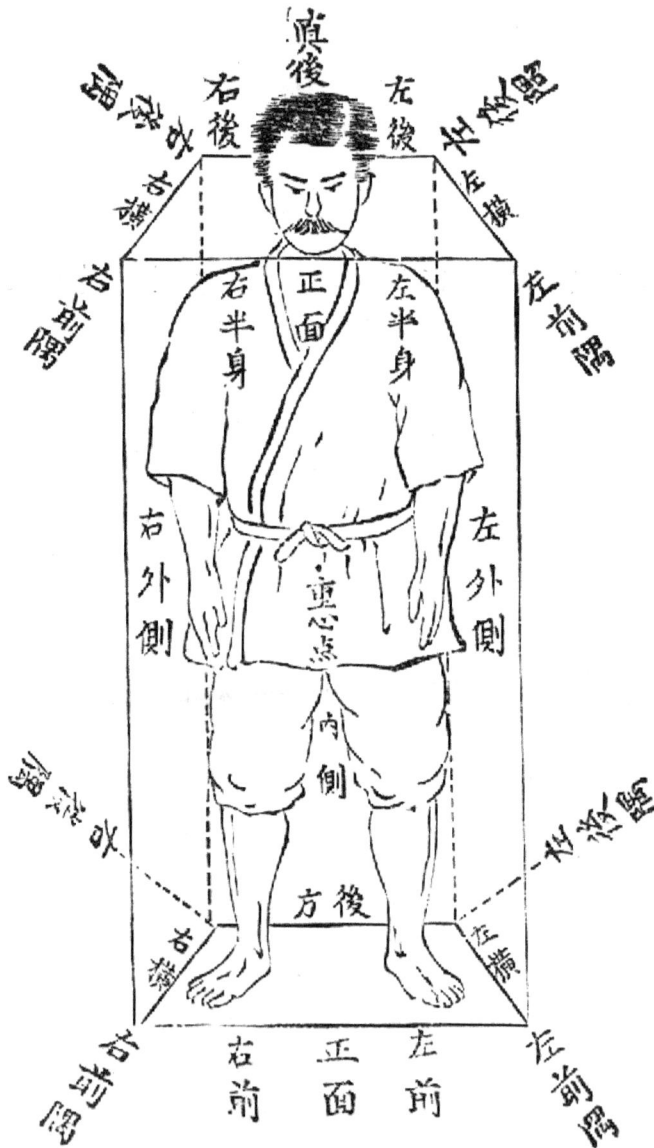

真後

右後　　左後

右後隅　　　左後隅

右横　　　　　　左横

右前隅　　　　　　左前隅

右半身　正面　左半身

右外側　　重心点　　左外側

内側

後方

右横　　　　　　左横

右前隅　　　　　　左前隅

右前　正面　左前

Illustration 7
Orientation of the Body

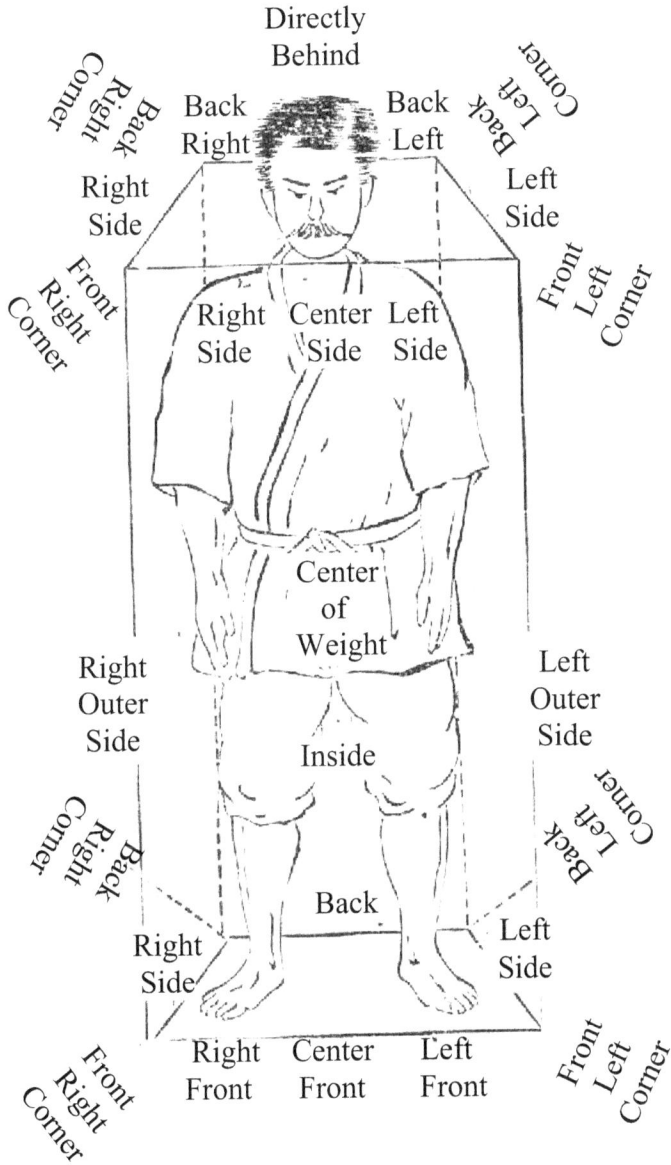

Directly
Behind

Right Corner Back

Back Left Corner

Back Right

Back Left

Right Side

Left Side

Front Right Corner

Front Left Corner

Right Side

Center Side

Left Side

Center
of
Weight

Right Outer Side

Left Outer Side

Inside

Back Right Corner

Back Left Corner

Back

Right Side

Left Side

Front Right Corner

Right Front

Center Front

Left Front

Front Left Corner

第八圖 敵を左前隅に釣込みたる所

我 *Ware* You	敵 *Teki* Opponent

第九圖 敵を右前隅に釣込みたる所

我
Ware
You

敵
Teki
Opponent

Forcing your opponent off balance on his Back Right Corner.

第十圖 敵を右後隅に崩したる所

敵 *Teki* Opponent	我 *Ware* You

#11
Forcing your opponent off balance on his Back Left Corner.

第十一圖 敵を左後隅に崩したる所

敵 *Teki* Opponent	我 *Ware* You

#12
Lifting your opponent forward and up.

第十二圖 敵を前に釣込みたる所

敵 *Teki* Opponent	我 *Ware* You

#13
Pushing your opponent backwards off balance.

第十三圖 敵を後に崩したる所

敵 *Teki* Opponent	我 *Ware* You

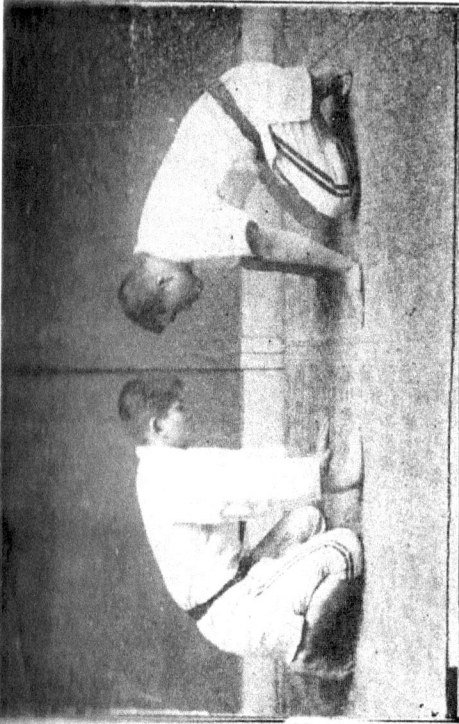

第十四圖 普通の禮

#14
Typical Rei (bowing in)

第十五圖 本式仕合の禮

#15
This style of Rei (bowing in) is used before an official duel.

#16
Stance before beginning an official duel.

第十六圖 本式仕合の構

#17
Shizen Hontai Main Natural Stance

第十七圖 自然本體

#18
Shizen Tai Natural Stance

第十八圖

自然體

#19
Jigo Hontai Self-Defense Stance

第十九圖　自護本體

#20
Migi Jigotai Right Self-Defense Stance

第二十圖右自護體

#21
Jotai no Kumikata, Typical Starting Position

第二十一圖 常體 の 組 方

#22
Yotsu no Kumikata Four-Handed Starting Position

#23
Hanmi no Kumikata Side on Starting Position

第二十三圖半身の組方

第二十四圖　仰向受身
#24
Aomuke Ukemi
Face up Break Fall

#25
Aomuke Ukemi
Face up Break Fall
Second Version

第二十五圖　同上別法

第二十六圖 俯伏受身

#26
Fuse Ukemi
Front Break Fall

第二十七圖 橫向受身

#27
Fuko Ukemi
SideBreak Fall

#28
The moment you attack with *Deashi Barai*,
Sweep the Front Foot.

第二十八圖 出足掃を掛けんとしたる瞬間

敵	我
Teki	*Ware*
Opponent	You

#29
This shows the positioning after *Deashi Barai*, Sweep the Front Foot. (In other words, the moment after the opponent is thrown.)

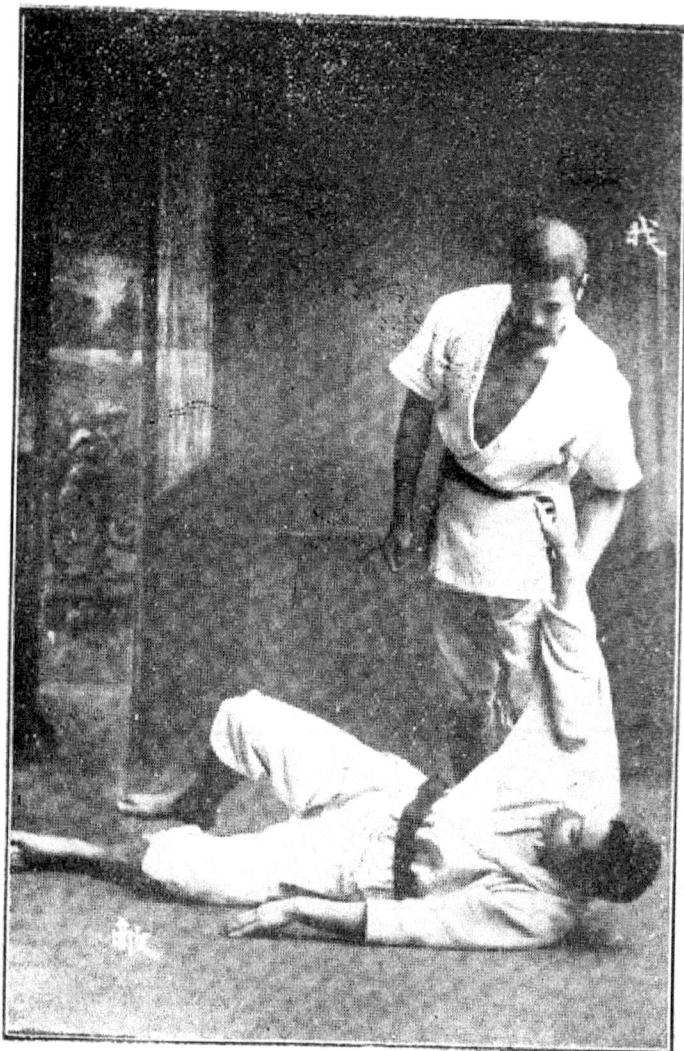

第二十九圖　同上掛けの終り（即ち投げたる瞬間）

敵 *Teki* Opponent	我 *Ware* You

#30
The moment you attack *Sasai Ashi*, Supporting Leg.

第三十圖

支足を掛けんとしたる瞬間

敵 *Teki* Opponent	我 *Ware* You

#31
Final move in *Tsubame Gaeshi,* Returning Kite
(This is, in other words, the moment you avoid the opponent's attempt to attack your leg.)

第三十一圖　燕返作りの終り（即ち敵の掃ひ足を避りたる瞬間）

敵 *Teki* Opponent	我 *Ware* You

#32
The moment you attack with *Tsubame Gaeshi*, Returning Kite.

第三十二圖 燕返を掛けたる瞬間

敵 *Teki* Opponent	我 *Ware* You

#33
The moment you attack with *Harai Ashi*, Foot Sweep.

第三十三圖　拂足を掛けんとしたる瞬間

敵 *Teki* Opponent	我 *Ware* You

#34
The moment you attack with *Hiza Guruma*, Knee Wheel.

第三十四圖

膝車を掛けんとする瞬間

敵 *Teki* Opponent	我 *Ware* You

#35
The moment you attack with *Okuri Harai*, Forward Sweep

第三十五圖　送掃を掛けんとする瞬間

我
Ware
You

敵
Teki
Opponent

#36
Picture showing after the sweep in #35.
(In other words the moment you toppled your opponent.)

第三十六圖　同上掛けの終り（即ち投げたる瞬間）

我	敵
Ware	*Teki*
You	Opponent

#37
The moment you attack with *Soto Gama*, Outer Sickle.

第三十七圖 外鎌を掛けんとする瞬間

敵
Teki
Opponent

我
Ware
You

#38
The moment you attack with *Uchi Gama*, Inner Sickle.

第三十八圖 内鎌を掛けんとする瞬間

我
Ware
You

敵
Teki
Opponent

#39
The moment you attack with *Yoko Wakare*, Side Separation.

第三十九圖 横分を掛けんとしたる瞬間

我 *Ware* You	敵 *Teki* Opponent

#40
The moment you attack with Y*oko Kake*, Side Attack.

第四十圖 横掛を掛けんとしたる瞬間

敵 *Teki* Opponent	我 *Ware* You

#41
Picture showing the end position after attacking with *Yoko Kake*, Side Attack.

| 我
Ware
You (background) | 敵
Teki
Opponent (foreground) |

#42
The moment you attack with Uki Waza, Floating Technique.

第四十二圖　浮業を掛けんとする瞬間

我	敵
Ware	*Teki*
You	Opponent

#43
The moment you have set up *Tsuri Komi Taoshi*, Lift and Topple.

第四十三圖　釣込倒の作りを終りたる瞬間

我 *Ware* You	敵 *Teki* Opponent

#44
The moment you attack with *Yoko Otoshi*, Side Drop.

第四十四圖 横落を掛けんとする瞬間

敵 *Teki* Opponent	我 *Ware* You

#45
Picture showing the position after you attacked with *Yoko Otoshi*, Side Drop.

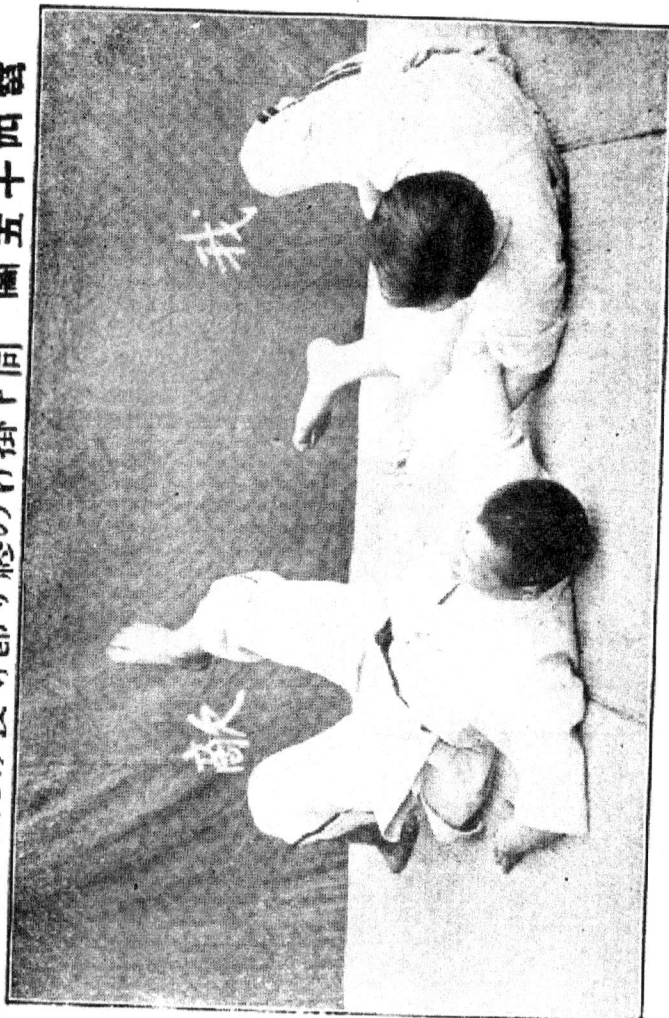

我	敵
Ware	*Teki*
You (right)	Opponent (left)

#46
Top: The moment you attack with *Tani Otoshi*, Valley Drop.
Bottom: Position after the throw.

第四十六圖

谷落を掛けんとする瞬間

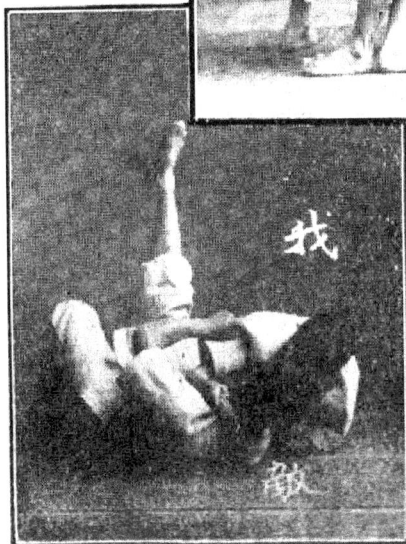

我

敵

同上掛けの終りたる瞬間

我

敵

敵 *Teki* Opponent (left)	我 *Ware* You (right)

#47
The moment you attack with an alternate version of
Tani Otoshi, Valley Drop.

四十七圖 同上別法を掛けんとする瞬間

敵 *Teki* Opponent	我 *Ware* You

#48
The moment you attack with a second alternate version of
Tani Otoshi, Valley Drop.

我 *Ware* You	敵 *Teki* Opponent

#49
The moment you attack with *Ura Nage*, Backwards Throw.

第四十九圖 裏投を掛けんとする瞬間

我	敵
Ware	*Teki*
You	Opponent

#50
Your position after finishing *Ura Nage,* Throw Back.

我	敵
Ware	*Teki*
You (right)	Opponent (left)

#51
Showing *Ushiro Goshi Kake*, Back Hip Attack, in mid-throw.
This is the moment you are readying to drop your opponent.

第五十一圖

後腰掛けの途中即ち敵を落さんとする瞬間

敵

我

我 *Ware* You	敵 *Teki* Opponent

#52
The moment you attack with *Yoko Guruma*, Side Car.

第五十二圖 横車を掛けんとする瞬間

敵
Teki
Opponent

我
Ware
You

#53
The moment you attack with *Daki Wakare*, Carry Away.

第五十三圖　抱分を掛けんとする瞬間

敵 *Teki* Opponent (bottom)	我 *Ware* You (top)

#54
The moment after you throw with *Daki Wakare*, Carry Away

第五十四圖　同上掛けの中途に即ち投げんとする瞬間

我	敵
Ware	*Teki*
You	Opponent

#55
The moment you throw with *Obi Otoshi Gake*, Belt Pick up & Drop.

第五十五圖帯落掛けの途中即投んとする瞬間

我 *Ware* You	敵 *Teki* Opponent

#56
Another version of *Obi Otoshi Gake*, Belt Pick up & Drop,
shown the moment you attack.

第五十六圖 帶落別法を掛けんとする瞬間

敵 *Teki* Opponent	我 *Ware* You

#57
Your positioning after throwing the variation of *Obi Otoshi Gake*, Belt Pick up & Drop, shown in picture #56.

敵 *Teki* Opponent (bottom)	我 *Ware* You (top)

#58
The moment you attack with *Sukui Nage*, Scoop & Throw.

第五十八圖 掬投を掛けんとする瞬間

敵	我
Teki	*Ware*
Opponent	You

#59
This shows your positioning mid-throw with *Sukui Nage*, Scoop & Throw.

第五十九圖　同上掛けの途中郎ち投げんとする瞬間

敵

我

敵 *Teki* Opponent	我 *Ware* You

#60
This shows your positioning after you set-up for *Tachiki Zoe*,
Alongside a Tree.

第六十圖 立木添の作りを終りたる瞬間

敵 *Teki* Opponent	我 *Ware* You

#61
This shows your positioning just before you throw with *Tachiki Zoe*, Alongside a Tree.

第六十一圖　同上掛けの途中即ち投げんとする瞬間

敵 *Teki* Opponent	我 *Ware* You

#62
This shows your positioning as you attack with Kani Sute, Crab Toss.

敵	我
Teki	*Ware*
Opponent (top)	You (bottom)

#63
This shows your positioning after you have set up *Tai Otoshi*, Body Drop.

第六十三圖　體落の作りを終りたる瞬間

敵 *Teki* Opponent	我 *Ware* You

#64
This shows your positioning mid-throw with *Tai Otoshi*, Body Drop.

第六十四圖　體落を掛けんとする瞬間

敵 *Teki* Opponent	我 *Ware* You

#65
This shows the moment you attack with *Uki Otoshi*, Float & Drop.

第六十五圖　浮落を掛けんとする瞬間

敵
Teki
Opponent

我
Ware
You

#66
This shows the moment you attack with *Soto Guruma*, Outer Wheel.

第六十六圖　外車を掛けんとする時間

敵
Teki
Opponent

我
Ware
You

#67
This shows the moment you attack with *Soto Guruma*, Outer Wheel.

第六十七圖　逆膝車を掛けんとする瞬間

敵	我
Teki	*Ware*
Opponent	You

#68
This shows the moment you attack with *Gyaku Game*, Reverse Sickle.

第六十八圖　逆鎌を掛けんとする瞬間

我 *Ware* You	敵 *Teki* Opponent

#69
This shows the moment you attack with Kama Goshi, Sickle Hips.

第六十九圖　鎌腰を掛けんとする瞬間

敵 *Teki* Opponent	我 *Ware* You

#70
This shows the moment you attack with *Okuri Gama*, Sending Sickle.

第七十圖

送鎌を掛けんとする瞬間

敵	我
Teki	*Ware*
Opponent	You

#71
The moment you attack with *Mune Taoshi*, Chest Throw.

第七十一圖　胸倒を掛けんとする瞬間

敵 *Teki* Opponent	我 *Ware* You

#72
The moment you attack with *Yama Arashi*, Mountain Storm.

敵 *Teki* Opponent	我 *Ware* You

#73
The moment when you attack with *Mata Otoshi*, Thigh Drop.

第七十三圖 股落を掛けんとする瞬間

敵 *Teki* Opponent	我 *Ware* You

#74
The moment you attack with *Ashi Guruma*, Leg Wheel.

敵 *Teki* Opponent	我 *Ware* You

#75
The moment you attack with *Soto Mata Harai*, Outside Thigh Sweep.

第七十五圖 外股拂を掛けんとする瞬間

敵 *Teki* Opponent	我 *Ware* You

#76
This shows your positioning mid-throw with *Uchi Mata Harai,*
Inside Thigh Sweep.

敵

我

第七十六圖　內股拂掛けの途中投げんとする瞬間

我	敵
Ware	*Teki*
You	Opponent

#77
The moment you attack with *Han Goshi*, Half Hip.

第七十七圖 半腰を掛けんとする瞬間

敵 *Teki* Opponent	我 *Ware* You

#78
This shows your positioning mid-throw with *Sukui Nage*, Scoop & Throw.

第七十八圖 同上掛けの終り即ち投げたる瞬間

我

敵

敵 *Teki* Opponent	我 *Ware* You

#79
The moment you attack with *Tsuri Goshi*, Fishing (lifting out) Hip.

第七十九圖　釣腰を掛けんとする瞬間

我 *Ware* You	敵 *Teki* Opponent

#80
The moment you attack with *Uki Goshi*, Floating Hip.

第八十圖 浮腰を掛けんとする瞬間

敵	我
Teki	*Ware*
Opponent	You

#81
This shows the mid-way point with *Uki Goshi*, Floating Hip.
You are about to drop your opponent.

第八十一圖 同上掛けの途中落さんとする瞬間

我

敵

敵 *Teki* Opponent	我 *Ware* You

#82
The moment you attack with *Tsuri Komi Koshi*,
Entering and Lifting Hip.

第八十二圖 釣込腰を掛けんとする瞬間

敵

我

敵	我
Teki	*Ware*
Opponent	You

#83
The moment you attack with *Hane Goshi*, Bounding Hip.

第八十三圖 跳腰を掛けんとする瞬間

我
Ware
You

敵
Teki
Opponent

#84
The moment you attack with *Hrai Goshi*, Sweeping Hip.

敵 *Teki* Opponent	我 *Ware* You

#85
This shows the set up for *Utsuri Goshi*, Moving Hip.

第八十五圖 移腰の作りを終りたる瞬間

我 *Ware* You	敵 *Teki* Opponent

#86
Continuing from #85, this shows the moment you throw with
Utsuri Goshi, Moving Hip..

第八十六圖

同上掛けんとする瞬間

敵

我

我 *Ware* You	敵 *Teki* Opponent

#87
The moment you attack with *Koshi Guruma*, Hip Wheel.

第八十七圖　腰車を掛けんとする瞬間

敵 *Teki* Opponent	我 *Ware* You

#88
An alternate way to attack with *Hane Goshi*, Bounding Hip.

第八十八圖　腰車別法を掛けんとする瞬間

敵 *Teki* Opponent	我 *Ware* You

#89
The moment you attack with *Ko Guruma*, Small Wheel.

第八十九圖 小車を掛けんとする瞬間

敵 *Teki* Opponent	我 *Ware* You

#90
Your position after you throw with *Ko Guruma*, Small Wheel.

第九十圖

同上掛けの終り即ち投げたる瞬間

我

敵

敵	我
Teki	*Ware*
Opponent (bottom)	You (top)

#91
The moment you attack with *Maki Komi*, Wrapping Up.

敵 *Teki* Opponent (left)	我 *Ware* You (right)

#92
Your final position after attacking with *Maki Komi*, Wrapping Up.

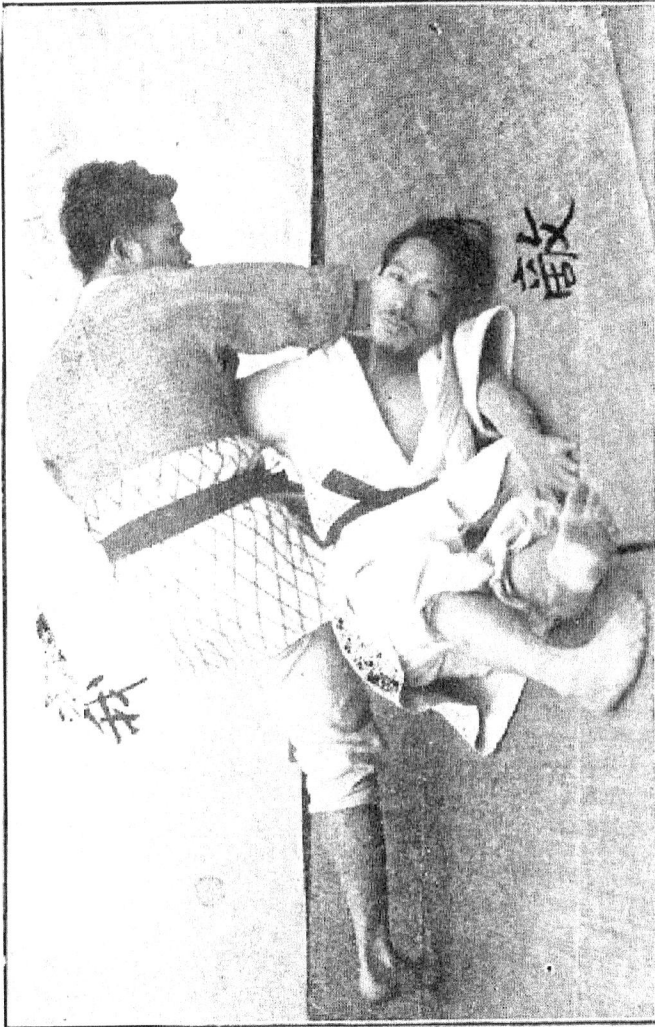

敵 *Teki* Opponent (bottom)	我 *Ware* You (top)

#93
The moment you attack with *Kata Otoshi*, Shoulder Drop.

第九十三圖 肩落を掛けんとする瞬間

敵 *Teki* Opponent	我 *Ware* You

#94
Your final position after attacking with *Kata Otoshi*, Shoulder Drop

我 *Ware* You	敵 *Teki* Opponent

#95
The moment you attack with *Seoi Nage,* Back Throw.

敵

我

第九十五圖 脊負投を掛けんとする瞬間

敵 *Teki* Opponent	我 *Ware* You

#96
The moment you attack with *Seoi Goshi,* Back Hip Throw.

第九十六圖 脊負腰を掛けんとする瞬間

敵
Teki
Opponent

我
Ware
You

#97
Your final position after attacking with *Seoi Goshi,*
Back Hip Throw.

第九十七圖 同上掛けを終りたる瞬間

我 *Ware*

敵 *Teki*

敵 *Teki* Opponent (bottom)	我 *Ware* You (top)

#98
The moment you attack with *Seoi Otoshi*, Back Drop.

第九十八圖 脊負落を掛けんとする瞬間

敵
Teki
Opponent

我
Ware
You

#99
The moment you attack with *Kinu Katsugi*,
Loading a Bale of Silk.

第九十九図　絹擔を掛けんとする瞬

敵 *Teki* Opponent (top)	我 *Ware* You (bottom)

#100
Your positioning after attacking with *Kinu Katsugi*,
Loading a Bale of Silk.

第百圖 同上掛けの終る即ち投げたる瞬間

敵	我
Teki	*Ware*
Opponent	You

#101
Another version of *Kinu Katsugi*,
Loading a Bale of Silk, shown mid-way through the attack.

第百一圖 絹擔別法掛けの途中

敵 *Teki* Opponent (top)	我 *Ware* You (bottom)

第　百　二　圖

間瞬るすんゝけ掛を投巴

#102 (above)
The moment you attack with *Tomoe Nage*, Spiraling Throw.

敵 *Teki* Opponent (top)
我 *Ware* You (bottom)

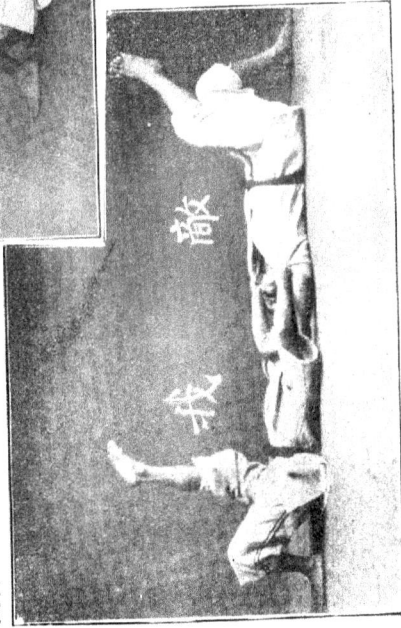

第　百　三　圖

間瞬るれゞ投ち卽ゝ終のゝ掛上同

#103 (below)
Your positioning after attacking with *Tomoe Nage*, Spiraling Throw.

敵 *Teki* Opponent (top)
我 *Ware* You (bottom)

第百四圖

所るれし放げ投く遠を敵てに投巴

#104 (above)
Attacking with *Tomoe Nage*, Spiraling Throw, will result in your opponent being thrown quite a distance.
敵 *Teki* Opponent (right)
我 *Ware* You (left)

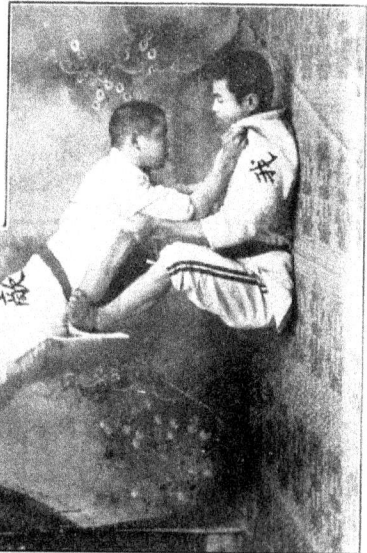

第百五圖

中途のけ掛巴本

#105 (right)
Attacking with *Hon Tomoe*, Main Spiraling Throw.
敵 *Teki* Opponent (top)
我 *Ware* You (bottom)

#104 (Detail)

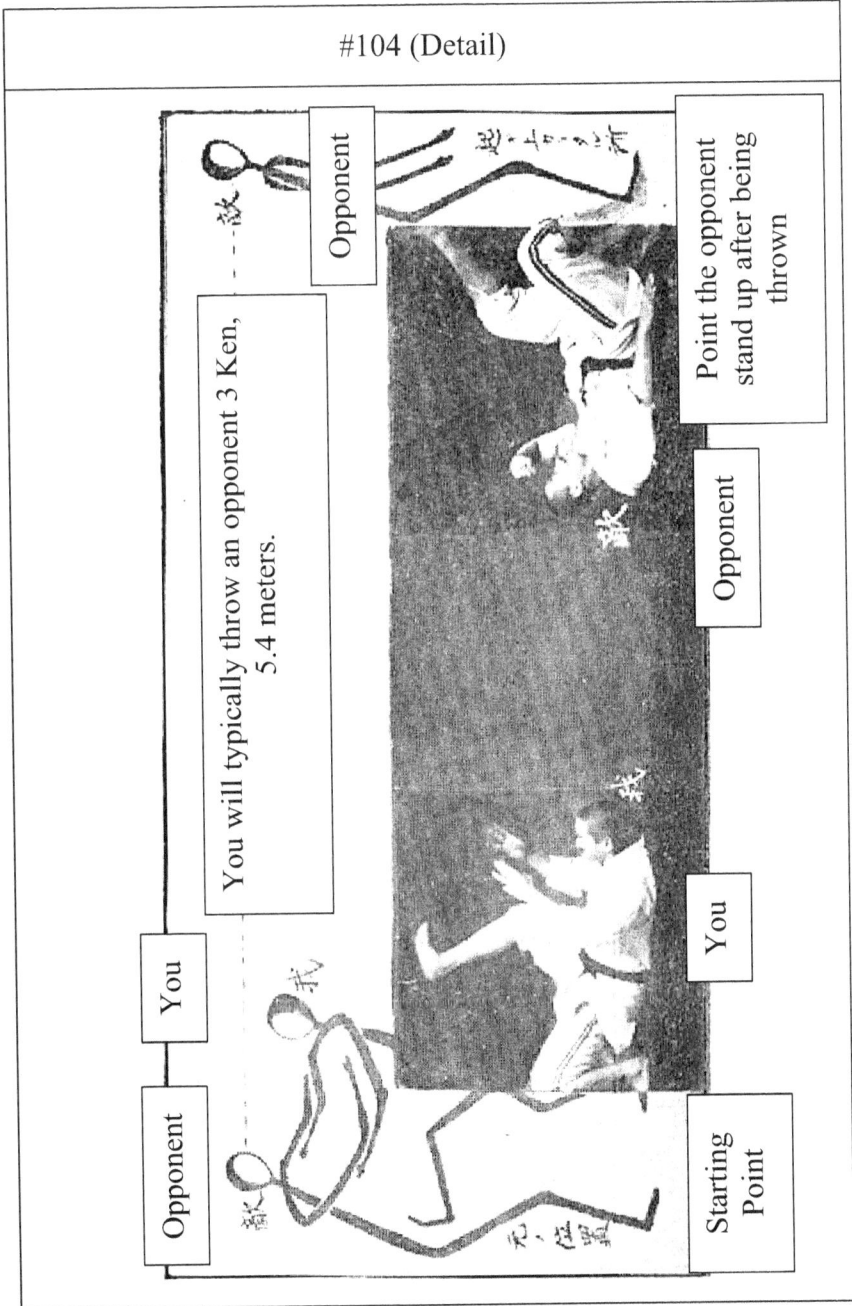

Opponent

Point the opponent stand up after being thrown

Opponent

You will typically throw an opponent 3 Ken, 5.4 meters.

You

You

Opponent

Starting Point

第百六圖

同上掛ぐらとんすゐる瞬間

#106 (above)

Position after attacking with *Hon Tomoe*, Main Spiraling Throw.

敵 *Teki* Opponent (right)

我 *Ware* You (left)

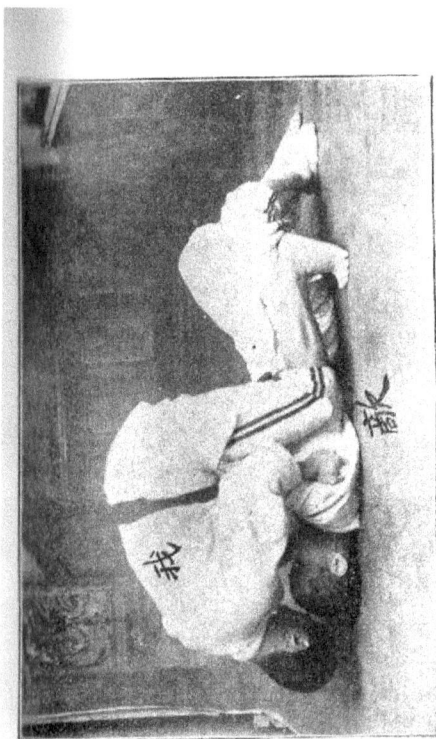

第百七圖

潜龍巴を捕げんとすゐる瞬間

#107 (below)

The moment you attack with *Sen Ryu Domoe*, Submerged Dragon Spiraling Throw.

敵 *Teki* Opponent (left) 我 *Ware* You (right)

#108
The moment you attack with *Sumi Kaeshi*, Returning Corner.

第百八圖 隅返を掛けんとする瞬間

我 *Ware* You	敵 *Teki* Opponent

#109
The moment you attack with *Tawara Gaeshi*,
Returning the Hay Bale.

第百九圖 俵返を掛けんとする瞬間

敵 *Teki* Opponent	我 *Ware* You

#110
The moment you attack with *Tsuri Otoshi,* Catch and Drop.

第百十圖 釣落を掛けんとする瞬間

敵	我
Teki	*Ware*
Opponent	You

#111
An example of a Newaza, Ground Fighting, attack. This shows
Semi-Iri, your opening attack.

後業攻例一の入り込める所

我
Ware
You (top)

敵
Teki
Opponent (bottom)

第百二十三圖

所る〳込へ抑て〵棒逆

#113 (below)
Suppressing your opponent with
Gyaku Tasuki, Sleeve Tie Lock.
敵 *Teki* Opponent (bottom)
我 *Ware* You (top)

第百二十二圖

所る〳込へ抑て〵棒固

#112 (above)
Suppressing your opponent with
Tasuki Katame, Sleeve Tie Lock.
敵 *Teki* Opponent (bottom)
我 *Ware* You (top)

第百十四圖

肩固て抑へ込みたる所

#114 (above)
Suppressing your opponent with
Kata Katame, Shoulder Lock.
敵 *Teki* Opponent (bottom)
我 *Ware* You (top)

第百十五圖

浮固て抑へ込みたる所

#115 (below)
Suppressing your opponent with
Uki Gatame, Floating Lock
敵 *Teki* Opponent (bottom)
我 *Ware* You (top)

第百六十圖

十字固てに抑へ込みたる所

#116 (above)
Suppressing your opponent with
Juji Katame, Cross Shaped Lock.
敵 *Teki* Opponent (bottom)
我 *Ware* You (top)

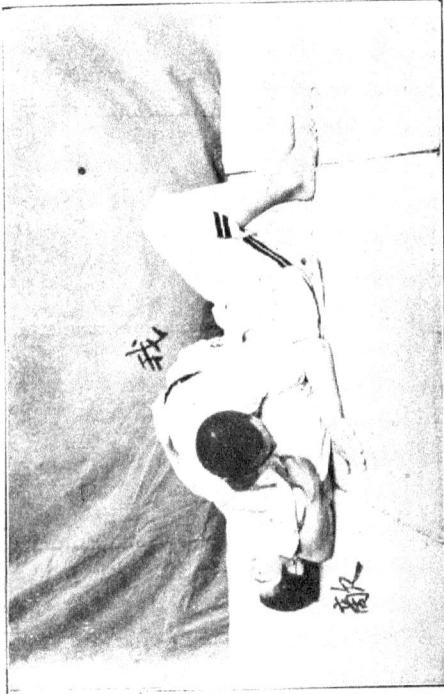

第百十七圖

四方固てに抑へ込みたる所

#117 (below)
Suppressing your opponent with
Shiho Katame, Four Direction Lock.
敵 *Teki* Opponent (bottom)
我 *Ware* You (top)

第百八十圖

崩四方に抑へ込み乃る所

#118 (above)
Suppressing your opponent with
Kuzure Shiho, Four Direction Break.
敵 *Teki* Opponent (bottom)
我 *Ware* You (top)

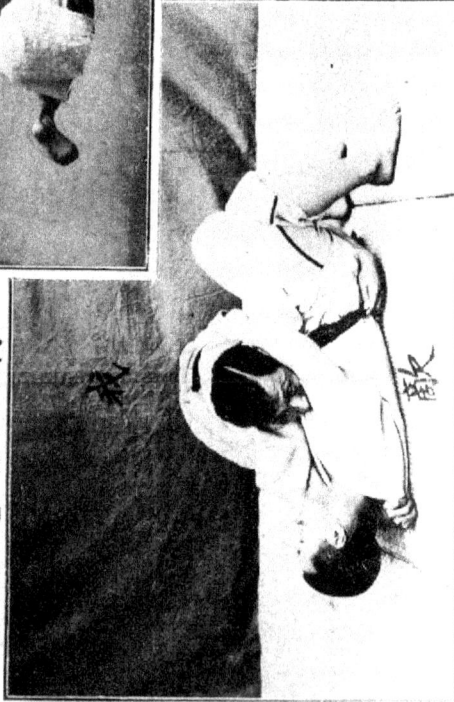

第百九十圖

閂固に抑へ込み乃る所

#119 (below)
Suppressing with *Kan-nuki Katame*,
Barring the Gates Lock.
敵 *Teki* Opponent (bottom)
我 *Ware* You (top)

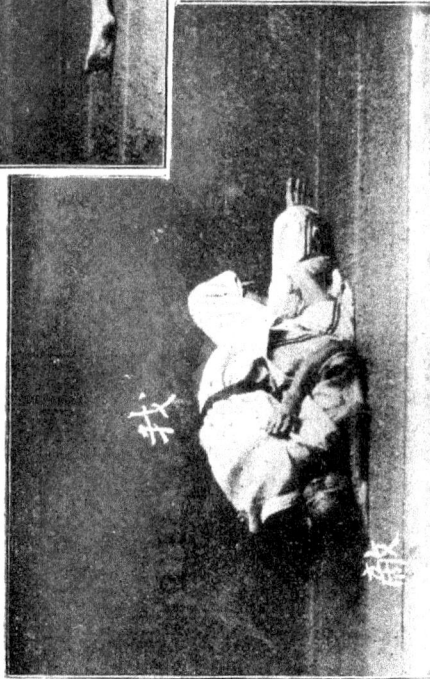

第百二十圖

後 に て 抑 込 れ る所

#120 (above)
Suppressing your opponent with
Ushiro Gatame, Back Lock.
敵 *Teki* Opponent (top)
我 *Ware* You (bottom)

#121 (below)
Suppressing with *Kari Gatame,*
Temporary Lock.
敵 *Teki* Opponent (bottom)
我 *Ware* You (top)

第百二十一圖

假 に て 抑 込 れ る所

#122
In the midst of attacking your opponent with
Nami Juji, Normal Cross Shaped Lock.

第百二十二圖　並十字及逆十字掛けの途中

敵	我
Teki	*Ware*
Opponent (bottom)	You (top)

#123
The first step of attacking your opponent with
Ushiro Juji, From Behind Cross Shaped Lock.

敵 *Teki* Opponent (bottom)	我 *Ware* You (top)

#124

Continuing to attack your opponent with
Ushiro Juji, From Behind Cross Shaped Lock.

第百二十四圖 同上掛けの途中

敵 *Teki* Opponent (bottom)	我 *Ware* You (top)

#125
In the midst of attacking your opponent with
Eri Shime, Collar Choke.

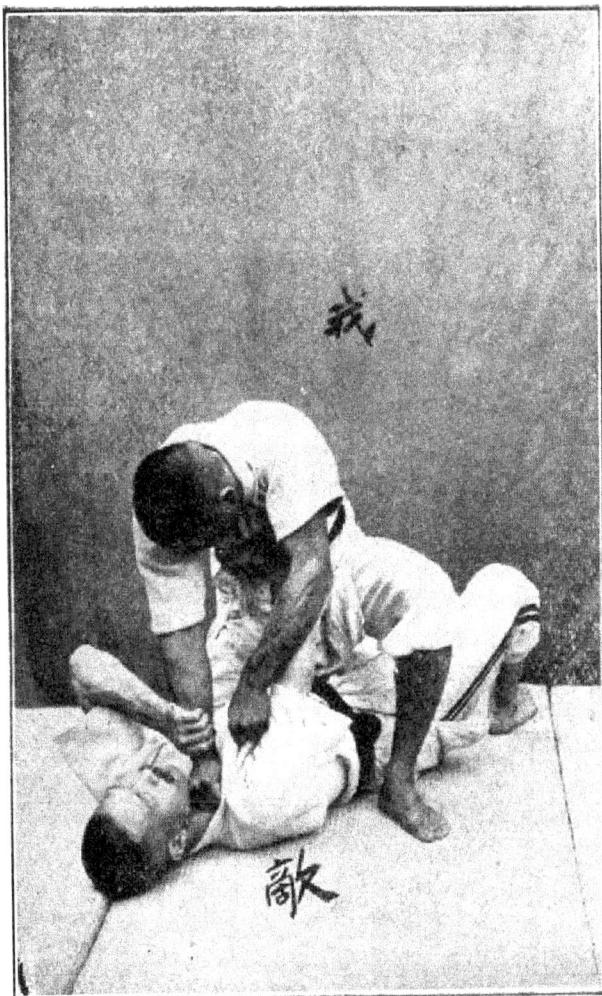

敵 *Teki* Opponent (bottom)	我 *Ware* You (top)

第二百二十六圖

中途のけ掛 襟 送

#126 (above)
In the midst of suppressing with
Okuri Eri, Sending Collar.
敵 *Teki* Opponent (bottom)
我 *Ware* You (top)

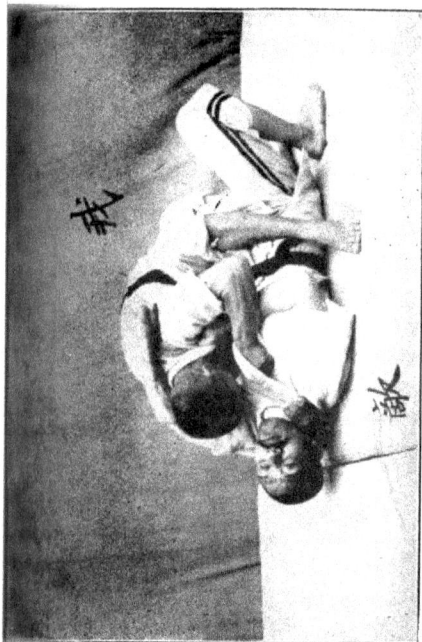

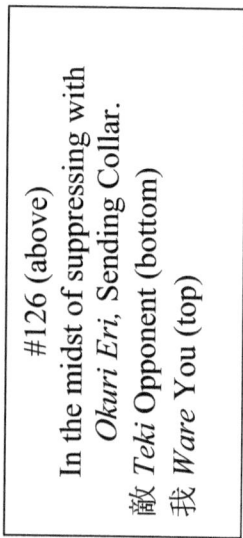

第二百二十七圖

中途のけ掛 絞 腕

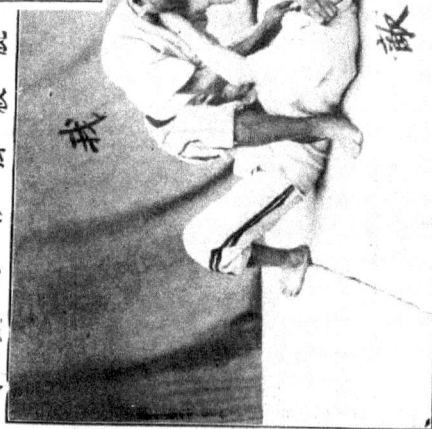

#127 (below)
In the midst of suppressing with
Ude Shime, Arm Choke.
敵 *Teki* Opponent (bottom)
我 *Ware* You (top)

#128
In the midst of attacking with *Yubi Shime*, Finger Choke.

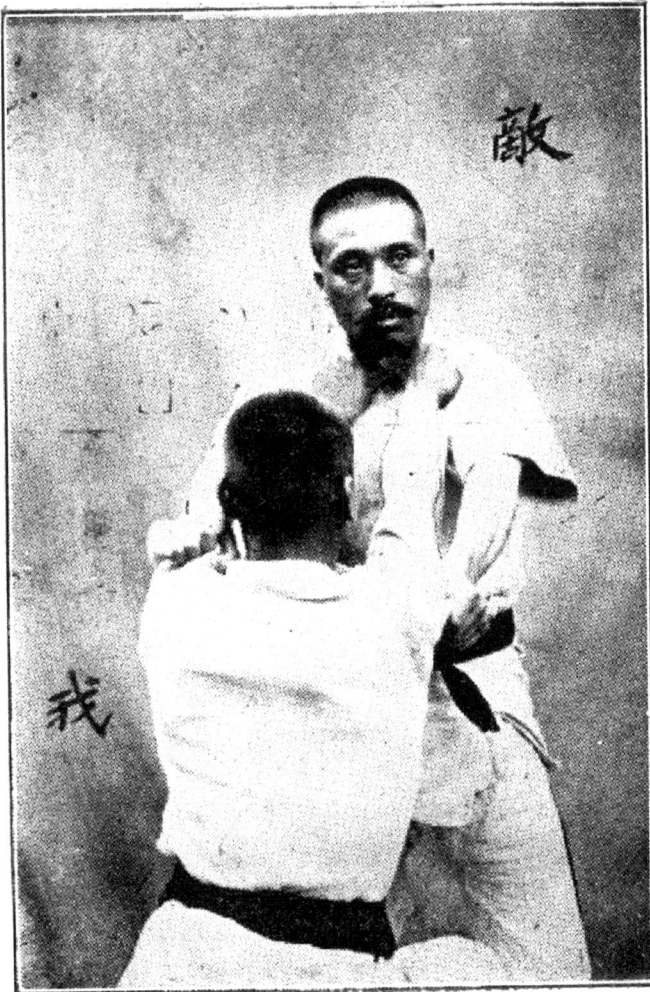

我	敵
Ware	*Teki*
You	Opponent

#129
In the midst of attacking with
Nigiri Shime, Gripping Choke.

第百二十九圖　握絞掛けの途中

我 *Ware* You	敵 *Teki* Opponent

#130
In the midst of attacking with
Kata Shime, Single Choke.

我	敵
Ware	*Teki*
You	Opponent

#131
In the midst of attacking with
Hadaka Shime, Naked Choke.

第百三十一圖 裸絞掛けの途中

敵	我
Teki	*Ware*
Opponent	You

#132
In the midst of attacking with another version of
Hadaka Shime, Naked Choke.

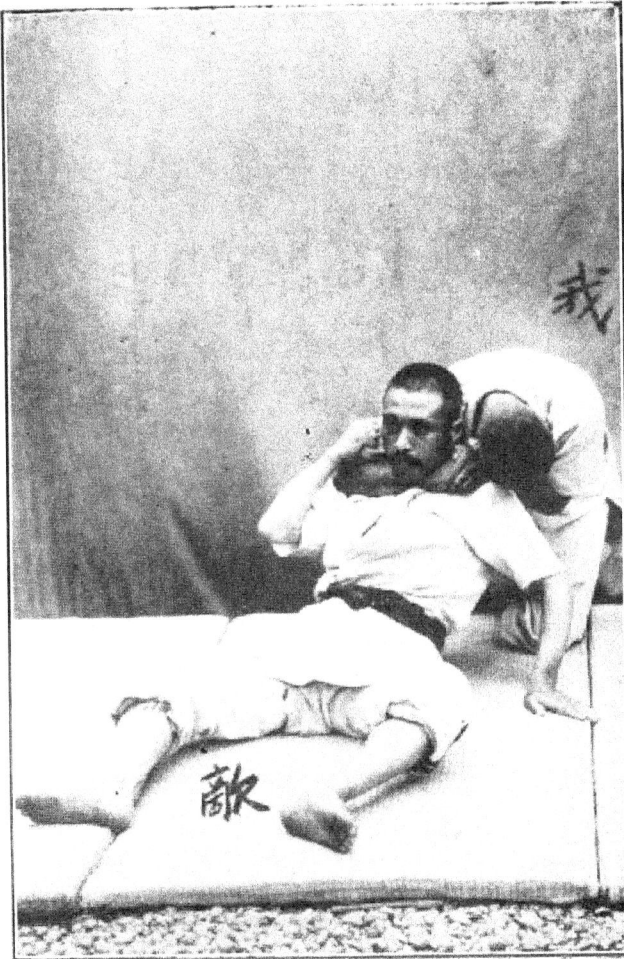

敵 *Teki* Opponent	我 *Ware* You

#133
In the midst of attacking with
Kata Ha Jime, Single Wing Choke.
Note: *Shime* and *Jime* are two readings for "choke" in Japanese.

第百三十三圖 片羽絞掛けの途中

我
Ware
You

敵
Teki
Opponent

#134
In the midst of attacking with
Haya Shime, Fast Choke.

敵	我
Teki	*Ware*
Opponent	You

#135
In the midst of attacking with *Tare Otoshi,* Hanging Drop.

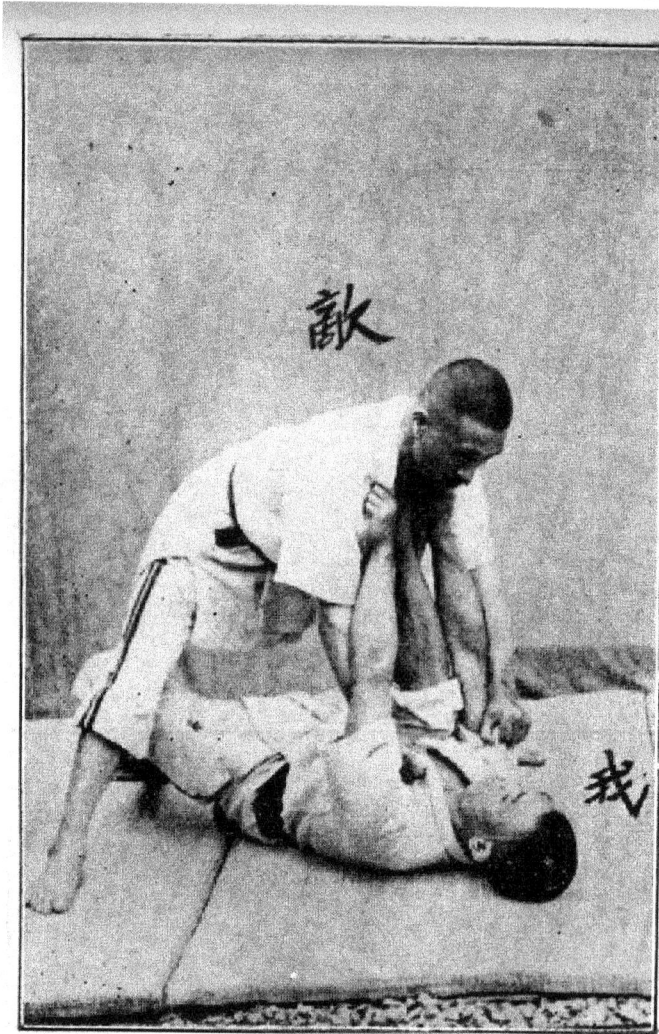

第百三十五圖 垂落掛けの途中

敵 *Teki* Opponent	我 *Ware* You

#136
In the midst of attacking with *Kubi Shigi,* Neck Breaker.

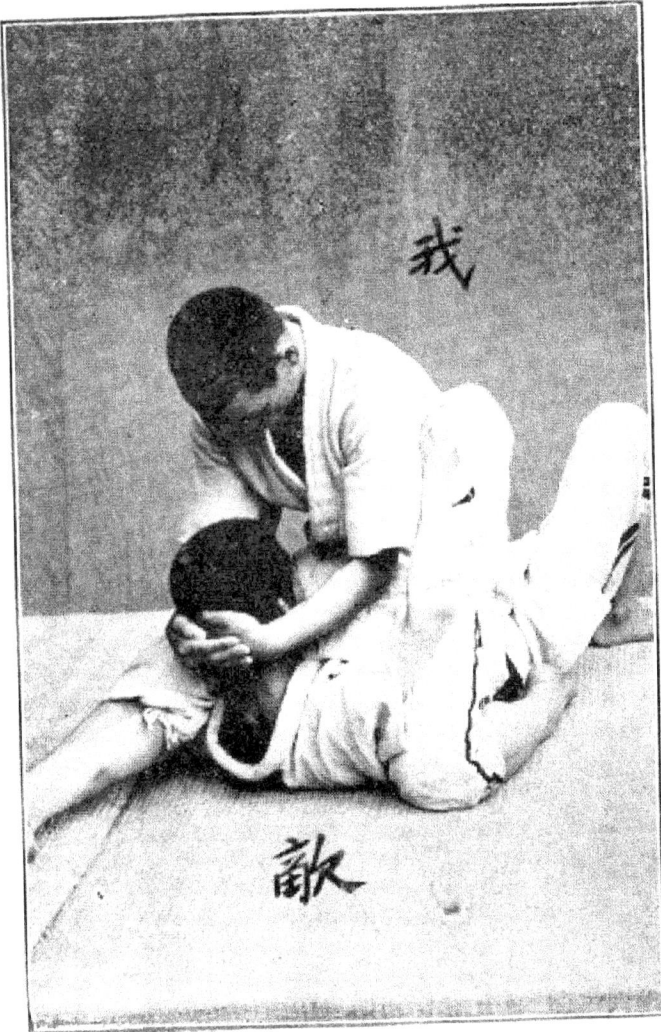

第百三十六圖 頸挫掛けの途中

我
Ware
You (top)

敵
Teki
Opponent (bottom

#137
Beginning your attack with *Ago Shime,* Jaw Choke.

第百三十七圖 頸締掛けの初め

我 *Ware* You	敵 *Teki* Opponent

#138
Continuing from the previous picture, this shows in the midst of attacking with *Ago Shime,* Jaw Choke.

| 敵
Teki
Opponent | 我
Ware
You |

#139
This shows in the midst of attacking with an alternate version of *Ago Shime,* Jaw Choke.

中途のけ掛法別上同 圖九十三百第

我 *Ware* You (top)	敵 *Teki* Opponent (bottom)

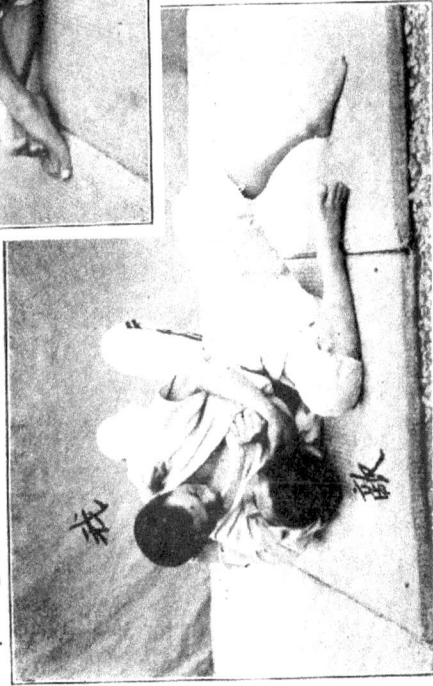

#140 (above)
In the midst of attacking with *Kubi Jime*, Neck Choke.
敵 *Teki* Opponent (bottom)
我 *Ware* You (top)

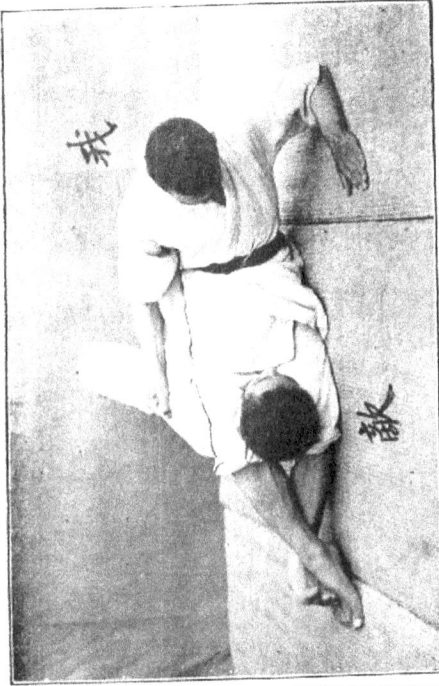

#141 (below)
In the midst of suppressing with *Daki Kubi*, Cradling the Neck.
敵 *Teki* Opponent (bottom)
我 *Ware* You (top)

In the midst of attacking with
Hiza Shime, Knee Choke.

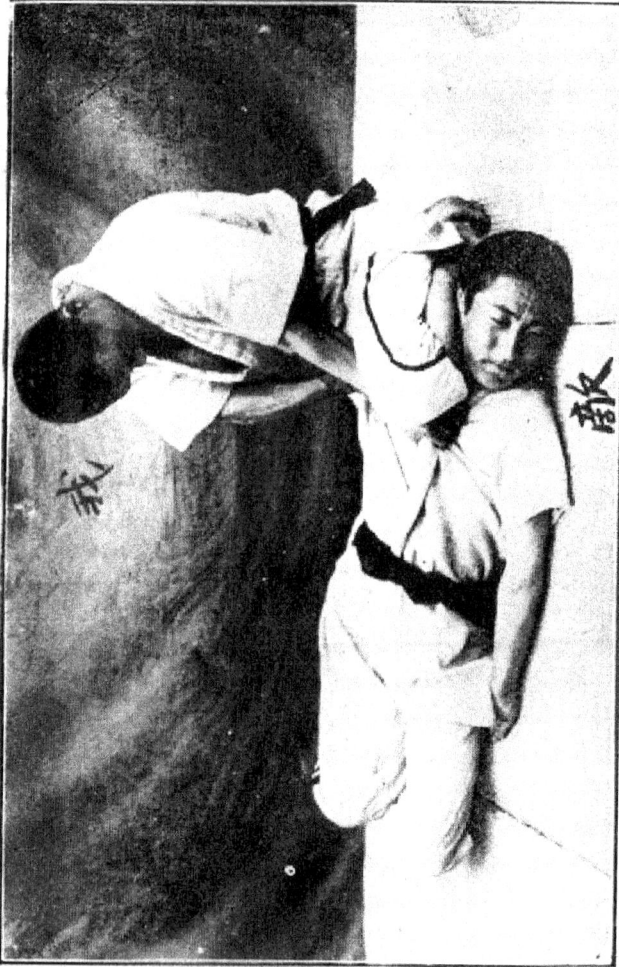

我 *Ware* You (top)	敵 *Teki* Opponent (bottom)

#143
In the midst of attacking with
Kubi Hineri, Neck Twist.

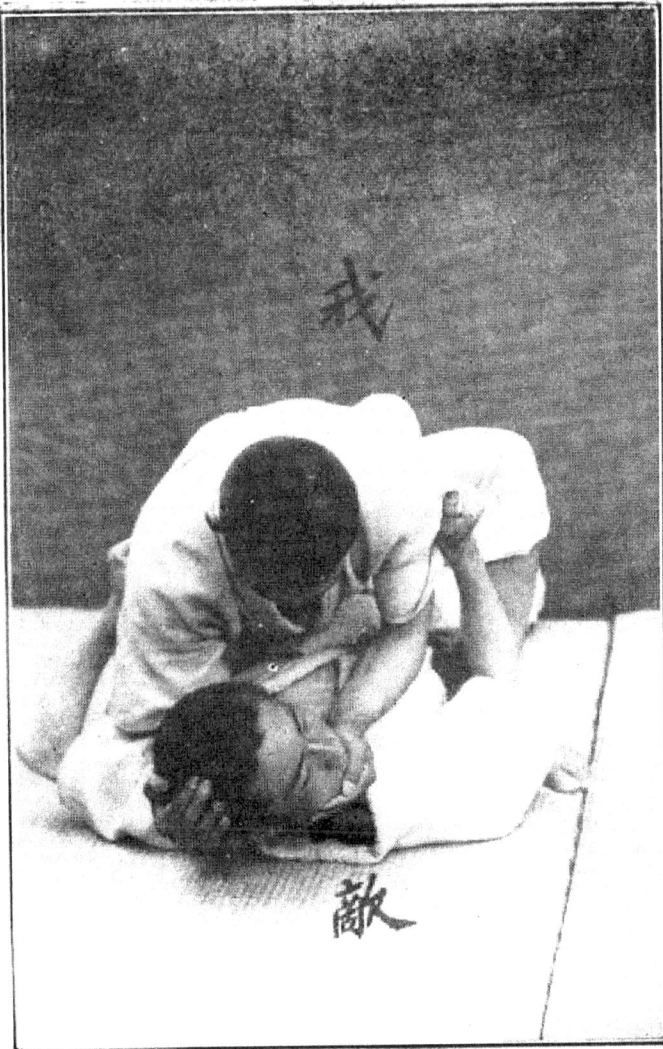

第百四十三圖 首捻掛けの途中

我	敵
Ware	*Teki*
You (top)	Opponent (bottom)

#144
In the midst of attacking with
Gyaku Yubi, Finger Reverse.

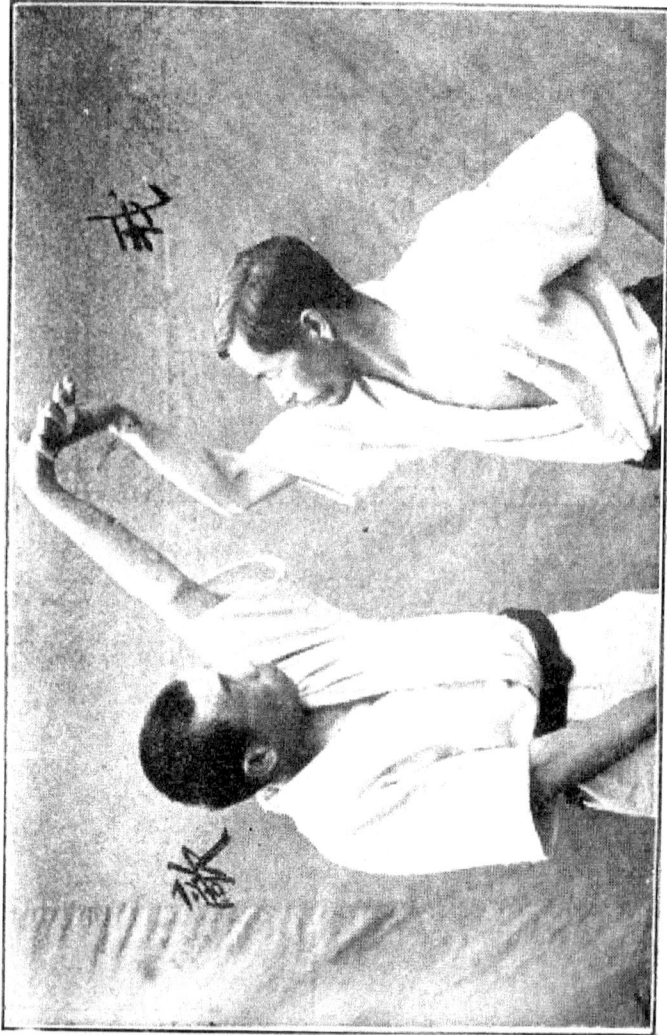

中途のけ掛指逆 圖四十四百第

我 *Ware* You (right)	敵 *Teki* Opponent (left)

#145
In the midst of attacking with
Kote Shigi, Breaking the Wrist.

我 *Ware* You	敵 *Teki* Opponent

#146
In the midst of attacking with
Uchi Kote, Inside Wrist.

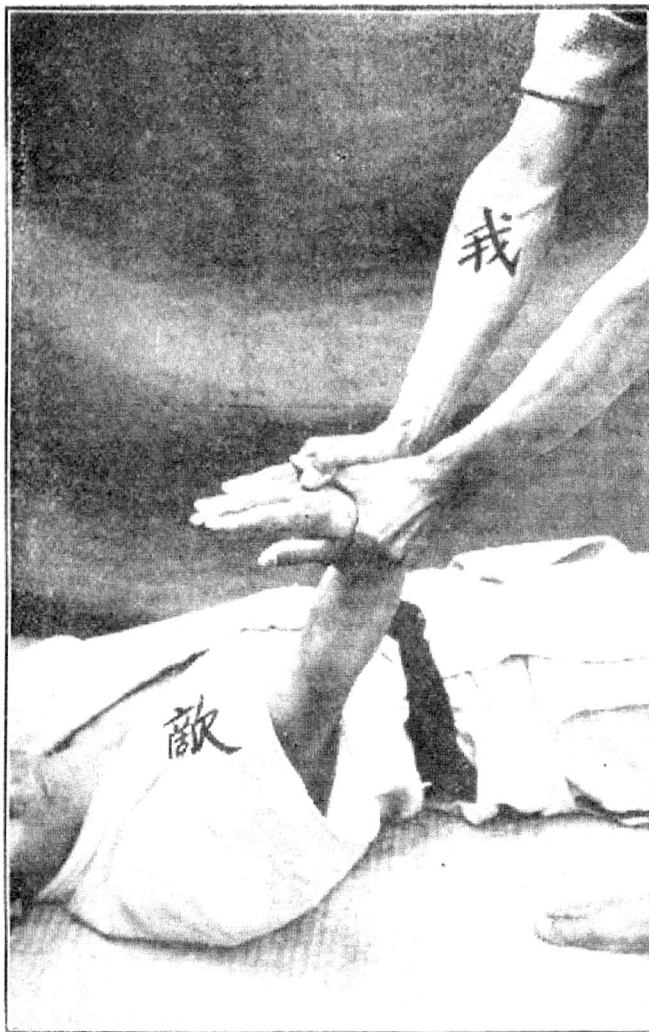

第百四十六圖 内小手掛けの途中

我
Ware
You

敵
Teki
Opponent

#147
Beginning your attack with
Kata Shime, Single Choke.

我 *Ware* You	敵 *Teki* Opponent

第百四十八圖

同上掛けの途中

#148 (above)
Suppressing your opponent with
Kata Shime, Single Choke.
敵 *Teki* Opponent (bottom)
我 *Ware* You (top)

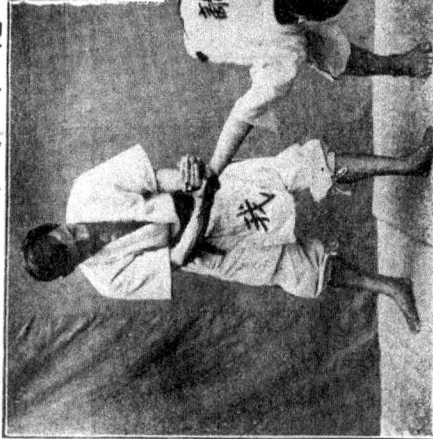

第百四十九圖

逆小手掛けの途中

#149 (below)
In the midst of suppressing with
Gyaku Kote, Wrist Reverse.
敵 *Teki* Opponent (bottom)
我 *Ware* You (top)

#150
In the midst of attacking with
Ude Karami, Arm Wrap.

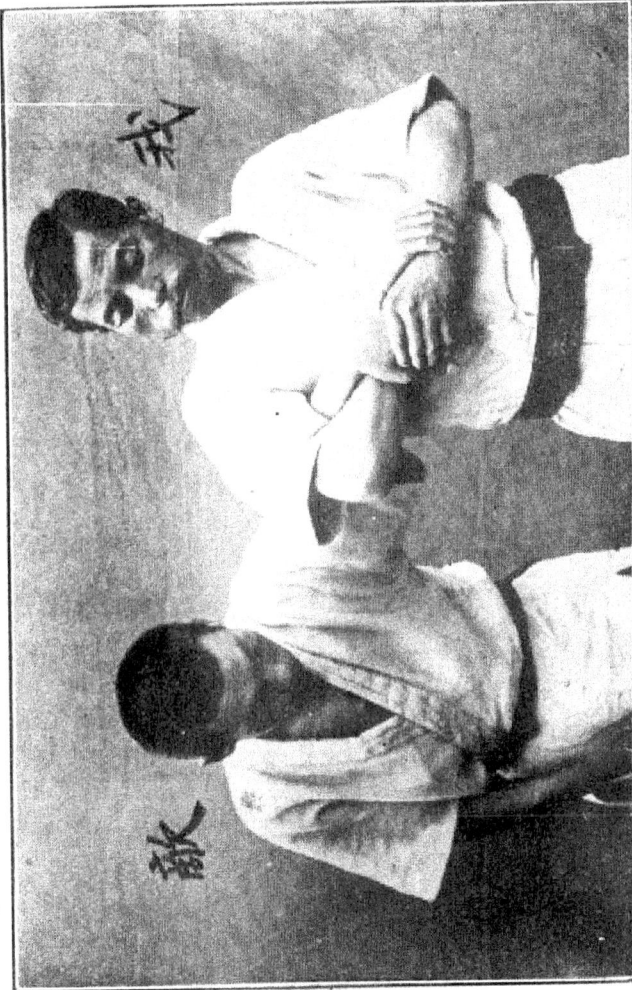

我	敵
Ware	*Teki*
You (right)	Opponent (left)

#151
In the midst of attacking with
Kata Shime, Single Choke.

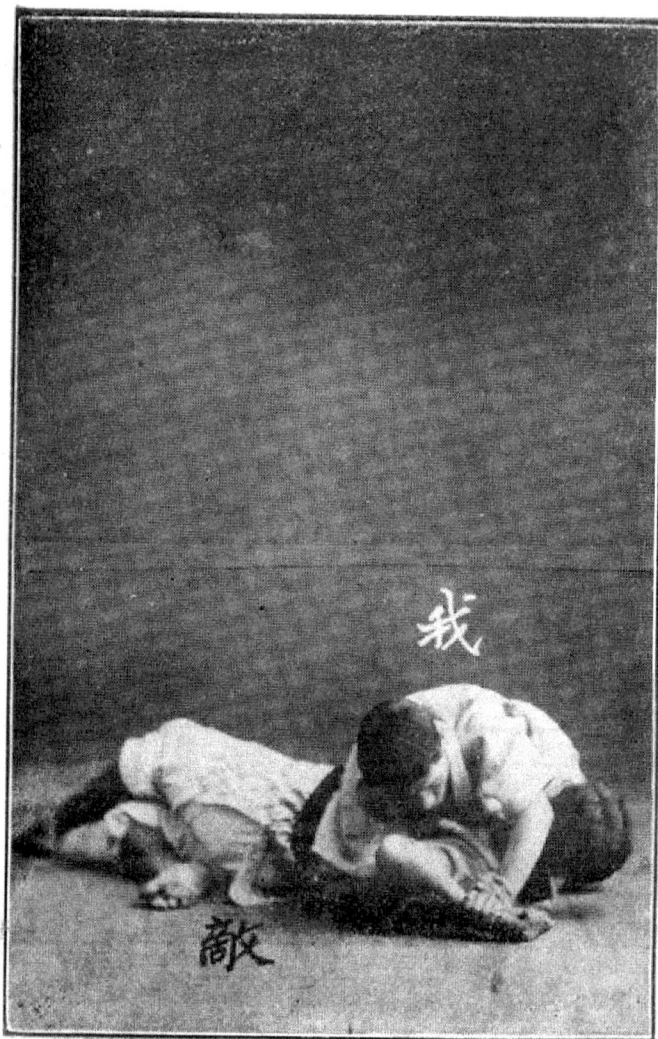

我	敵
Ware	*Teki*
You (top)	Opponent (bottom)

#152
Beginning your attack with
Enma, Lord of the Underworld.

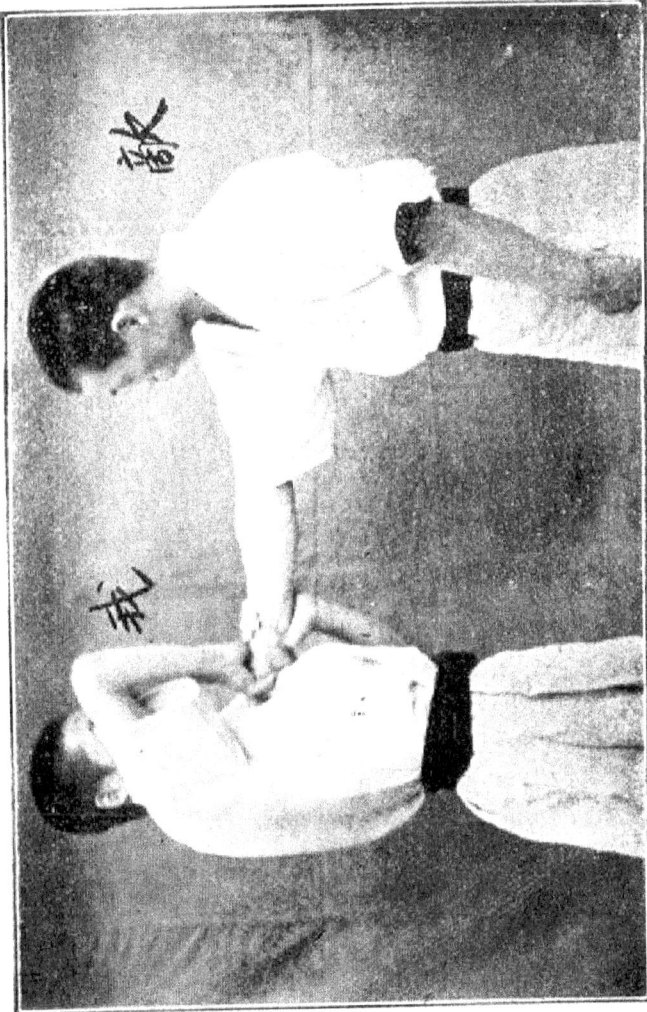

第百五十二圖 閻魔掛けの初め

我 *Ware* You (right)	敵 *Teki* Opponent (left)

#153
In the midst of attacking with
Enma, Lord of the Underworld.

第百五十三圖 同上掛けの途中

我 *Ware* You	敵 *Teki* Opponent

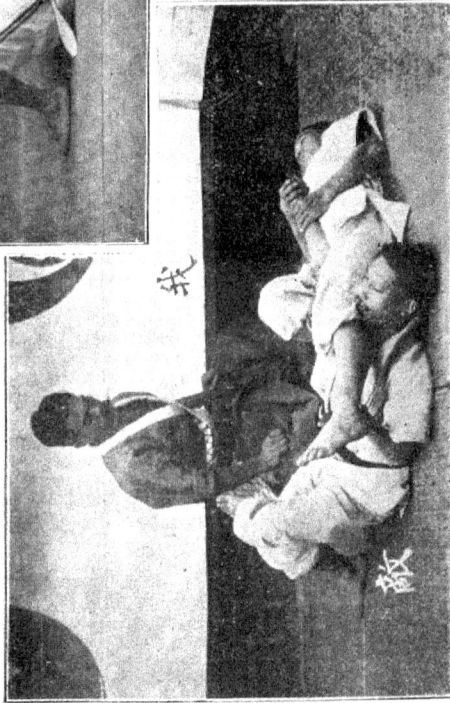

肱挫け掛五百十四圖

初めの

#154 (above)
Beginning your attack with
Ude Shigi, Arm Break.
敵 *Teki* Opponent (bottom)
我 *Ware* You (top)

第百五十五圖

同上 掛けの途中

#155 (below)
In the midst of suppressing with
Ude Shigi, Arm Break.
敵 *Teki* Opponent (bottom)
我 *Ware* You (top)

第百五十六圖

膝固腕固け掛の途中

#156 (above)
In the midst of suppressing with
Hiza Katame Ude Shigi, Locking the
Knee and Breaking the Arm.
敵 *Teki* Opponent (bottom)
我 *Ware* You (top)

第百五十七圖

腕固挫腕け掛の途中

#157 (below)
Another photograph showing you in the
midst of suppressing with
Ude Katame Ude Shigi,
Locking the Arm and breaking the Arm.
敵 *Teki* Opponent (bottom)
我 *Ware* You (top)

#158
Another photograph showing you in the midst of suppressing
with *Ude Katame Ude Shigi,*
Locking the Arm and Breaking the Arm.

我 *Ware* You	敵 *Teki* Opponent

#159
In the midst of attacking with
Tachi Ude Shigi, Standing Arm Break.

第百五十九圖 立腕挫掛けの途中

敵	我
Teki	*Ware*
Opponent	You

第百六十圖

胴絞作りの途中

#160 (above)
In the midst of suppressing with
Do Jime, Waist Choke.
敵 *Teki* Opponent (bottom)
我 *Ware* You (top)

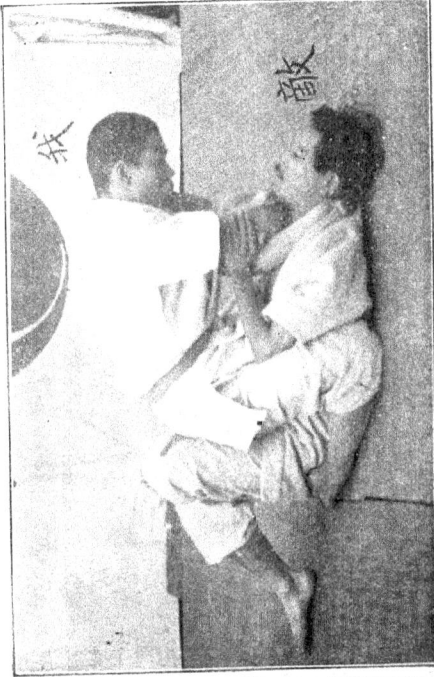

同上掛けの途中

第百六十一圖

#161 (below)
Another picture showing you applying
Do Jime, Waist Choke.
敵 *Teki* Opponent (bottom)
我 *Ware* You (top)

#162

In the midst of attacking with
Do Goroshi, Killing the Waist.

第百六十二圖　胴殺掛けの途中

敵
Teki
Opponent

我
Ware
You

#163
In the midst of attacking with
Mune Otoshi, Chest Drop.

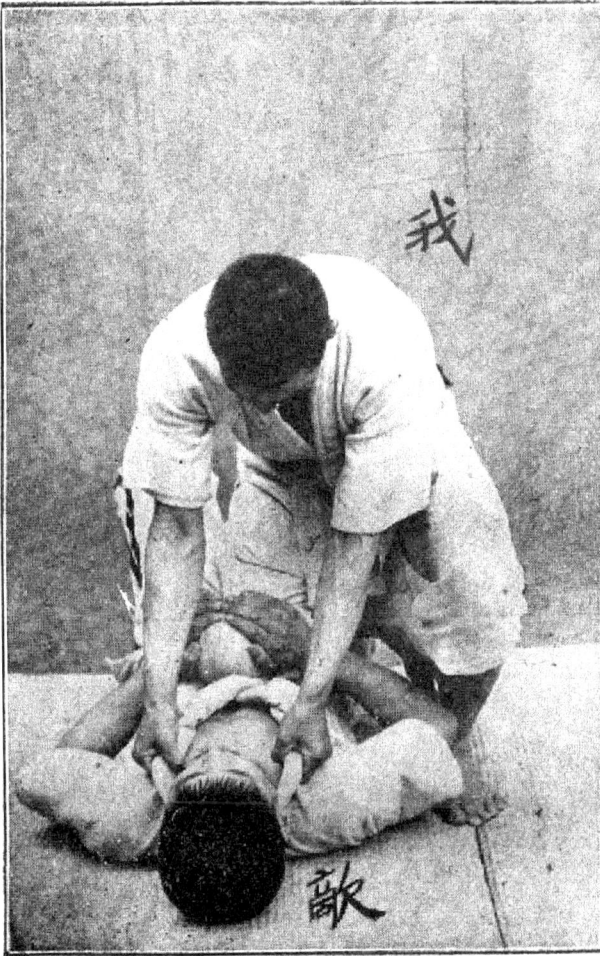

第百六十三圖　胸落掛けの途中

我
Ware
You (top)

敵
Teki
Opponent (bottom)

#164
In the midst of attacking with
Se Shigi, Backbreaker.

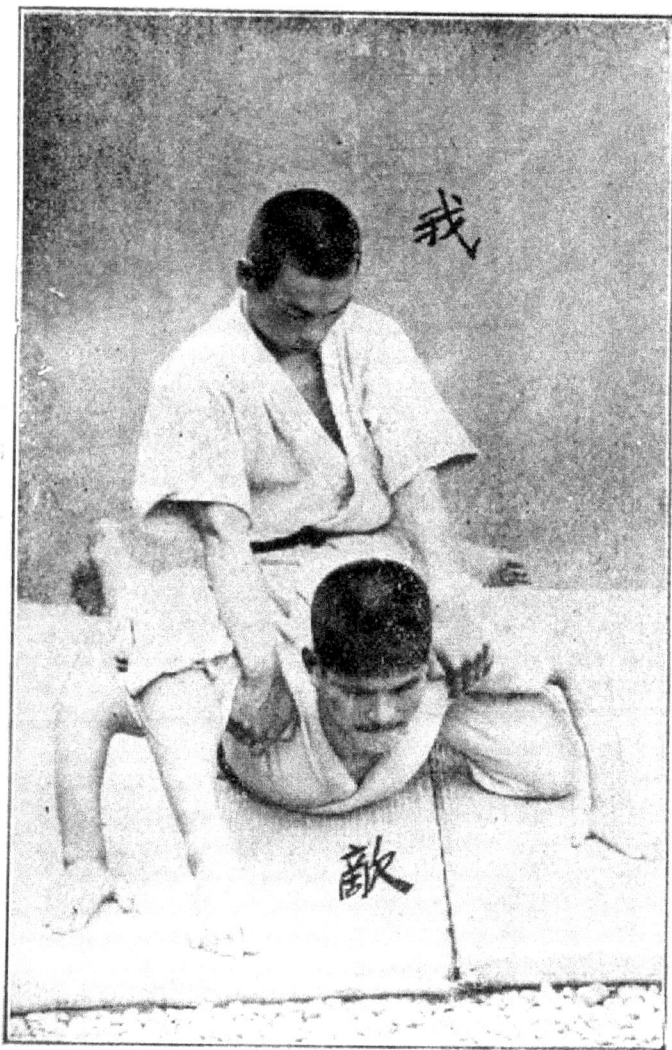

第百六十四圖 脊挫掛けの途中

我	敵
Ware	*Teki*
You (top)	Opponent (bottom)

#165
In the midst of attacking with
Koshi Shigi, Hip Breaker.

我	敵
Ware	*Teki*
You (top)	Opponent (bottom)

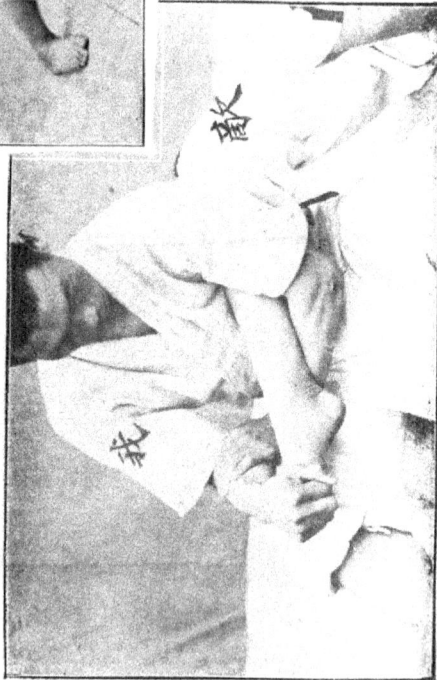

第百六十六圖

海老締め掛けの途中

#166 (above)
In the midst of suppressing with
Ebi Jime, Shrimp Choke.
敵 *Teki* Opponent (bottom)
我 *Ware* You (top)

#167 (below)
In the midst of suppressing with
Yubi Zume, Toe Compression.
敵 *Teki* Opponent (bottom)
我 *Ware* You (top)

第百六十七圖

指詰め掛けの途中

第百六十八圖
足　挫　け　の　途　中

#168 (above)
In the midst of suppressing with
Ashi Shigi, Leg Break.
敵 *Teki* Opponent (left)
我 *Ware* You (right)

第百六十九圖
足　捻　け　の　途　中

#169 (below)
In the midst of suppressing with
Ashi Yori, Leg Twist.
敵 *Teki* Opponent (left)
我 *Ware* You (right)

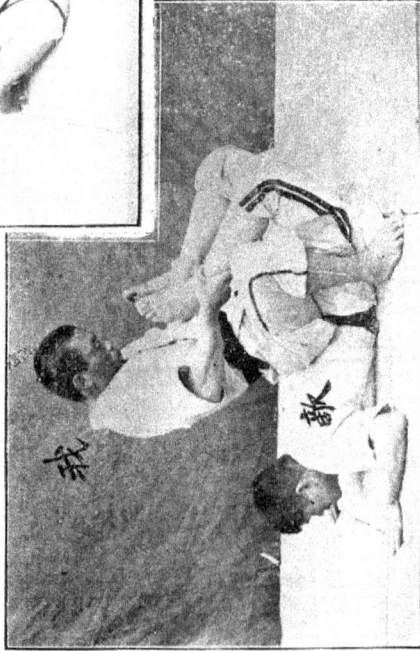

第百七十圖

中途のけ掛絞股

#170 (above)
In the midst of suppressing with
Mata Jime, Thigh Choke.
敵 *Teki* Opponent (bottom)
我 *Ware* You (top)

第百七十一圖

中途のけ掛絞裏

#171 (below)
In the midst of suppressing with
Ura Jime Reverse Choke also known as
Shachi Jime, Killer Whale Choke.
敵 *Teki* Opponent (bottom)
我 *Ware* You (top)

162

#172
In the midst of attacking with
Ashi Garami, Leg Entangler.

我	敵
Ware	*Teki*
You (bottom)	Opponent (top)

#173
Continuing your attack with
Ashi Garami, Leg Entangler.

第百七十三圖　同上掛けの途中

我 *Ware* You	敵 *Teki* Opponent

#174
In the midst of attacking with *Ashi Garami,* Leg Entangler.
Note: The name is the same but the Kanji differ. This version
attacks both muscle and joints, whereas the previous technique
focuses on joints.

中途のけ掛繆足　圖四十七百第

我	敵
Ware	*Teki*
You (top)	Opponent (bottom)

#175
How to position your arms and hands for
Shime Waza, Choke Technique.

第百七十五圖　締技の抱手應用

敵 *Teki* Opponent	我 *Ware* You

#176
Kyusho, Vital Points, on the front of the body.

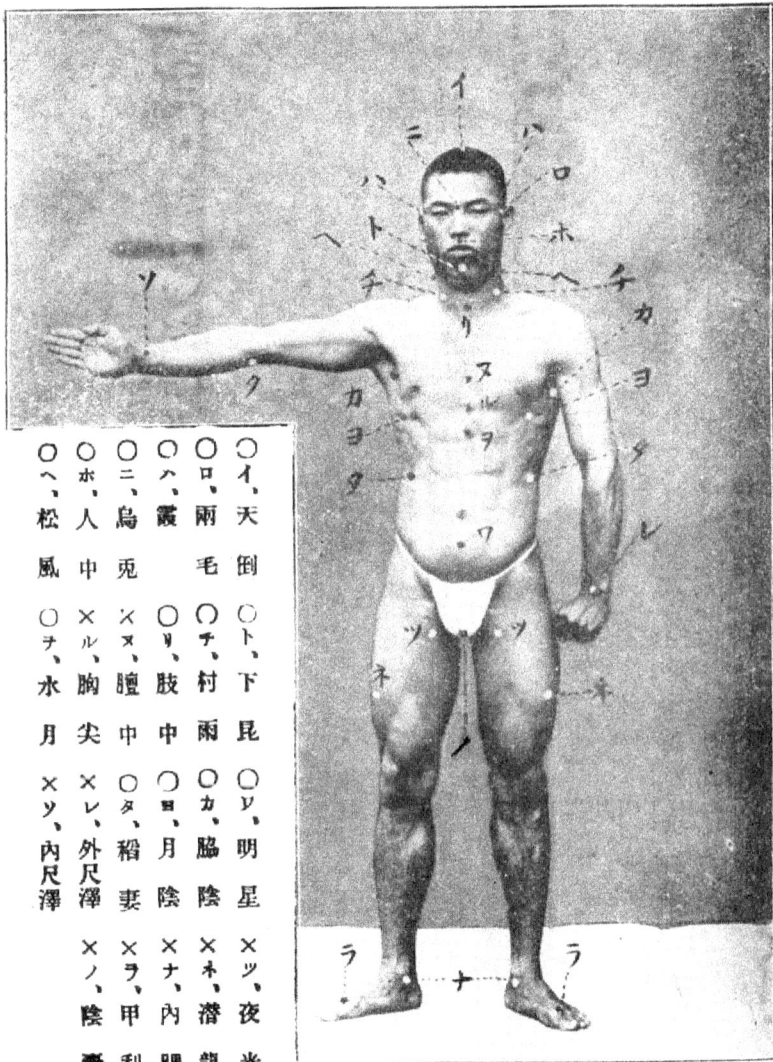

面前所急體人　圖六十七百第

Kyusho, Vital Points, on the back of the body.

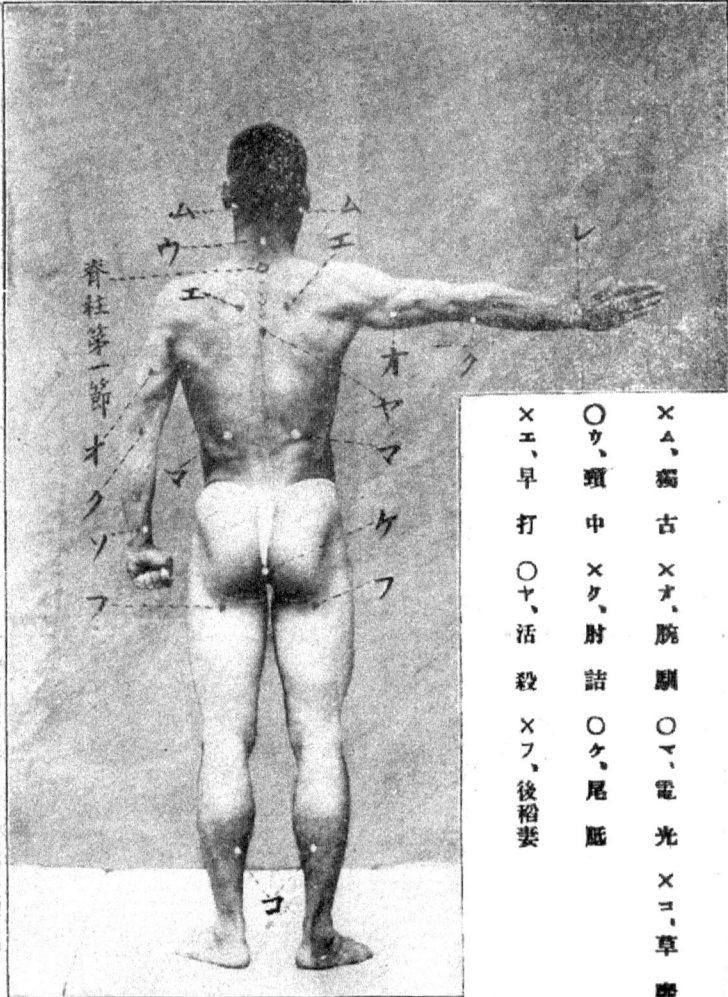

人體急所後面　　第百七十七圖

×ム、髑古　×オ、腕賵　○マ、電光　×コ、草鹿

○ウ、頸中　×タ、肘詰　○ケ、尾骶

×エ、早打　○ヤ、活殺　×フ、後稻妻

168

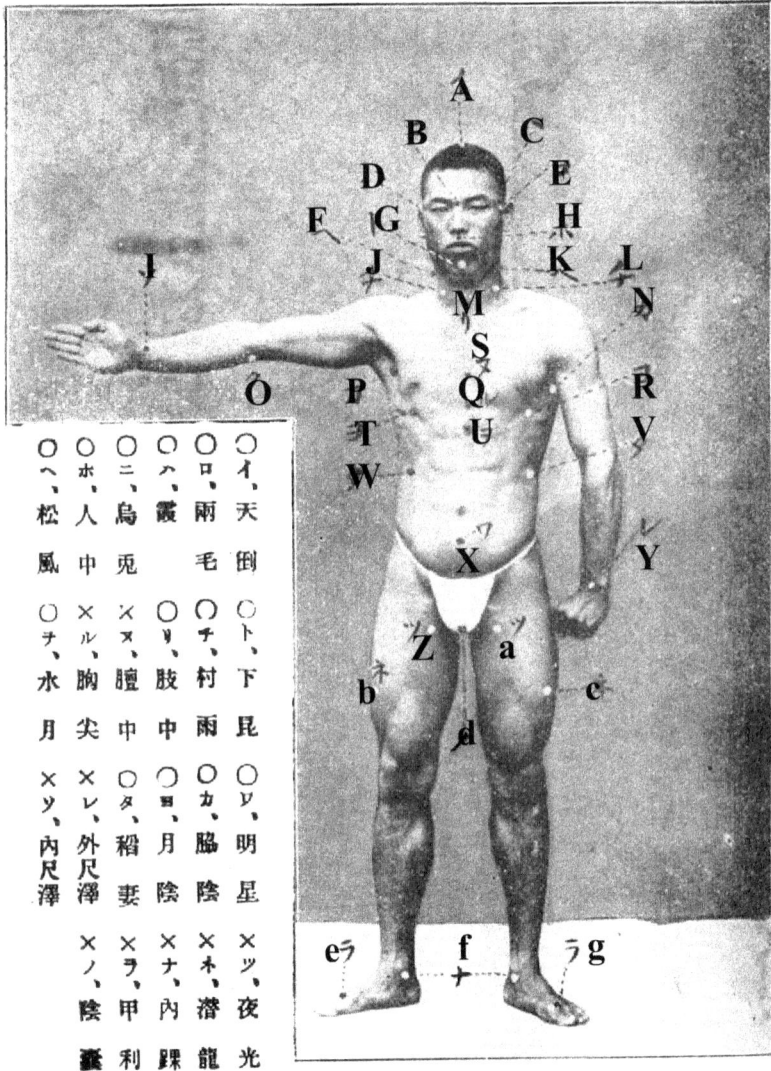

第百七十六圖　人體急所前面

○ヘ、松風	○ホ、人中	○ニ、烏兎	○ハ、霞	○ロ、兩毛	○イ、天倒			
○ナ、水月	×ル、胸尖	×ヌ、膻中	×リ、肢中	○チ、村雨	○ト、下昆			
×ツ、内尺澤	×レ、外尺澤	○タ、稲妻	○ヨ、月陰	○カ、脇陰	○ソ、明星			
	×ノ、陰囊	×ヲ、甲利	×ナ、内踝	×ネ、潛龍	×ツ、夜光			

169

Translator's Note:
The following charts show Kyusho, Vital Points. The readings and meanings of the points on this chart are all approximate. There is an additional indication of ○ or × above each point.
○ Striking this point with sufficient force will result in *Sokushi* 即死 Sudden Death.
× Striking this point with sufficient force will result in *Sokutoh* 即倒 Sudden Incapacitation

○ヘ、霞 ○ヌ、肢中 ○ヨ、月陰 ×ナ、內踝	D ○ *Kasumi* Mist	○ロ、兩毛 ○チ、村雨 ○カ、脇陰 ×ネ、潜龍	E ○ *Ryoke* Both Hair	○イ、天倒 ○ト、下昆 ○ル、明星 ×ツ、夜光	A ○ *Tentoh* Heavan Topple
	M ○ *Shichu* Center of Limbs		J ○ *Murasame* Village Rain		G ○ *Kakon* Lower Insect
	R × *Gekkage* Shadow of the Moon		P ○ *Waki Kage* Side Shadow		X ○ *Myosei* Bright Star
	f × *Naika* Inner Ankle		b,c × *Senryu* Submerged Dragon		Z,a × *Yakoh* Darkness and Light

〇イ、天倒
〇ト、下昆
〇レ、明星
×ツ、夜光

〇ロ、兩毛
〇チ、村雨
〇ネ、潜龍
×ナ、內踝

〇ハ、霞
〇リ、肢中
〇カ、脇陰
×ラ、甲利

〇ニ、烏兎
×ヌ、膻中
〇ヨ、月陰
×タ、稻妻

×ヌ、胸尖
×レ、外尺澤
×ノ、陰囊

〇ホ、人中
×ル、胸尖
×レ、外尺澤

〇ヘ、松風
〇チ、水月
×ツ、內尺澤

○ *Sokushi* 即死 Sudden Death.

× *Sokutoh* 即倒 Sudden Incapacitation.

○ヘ、松風 ○チ、水月 ×ツ、内尺澤	K ○ *Matsukaze* Wind in the Pines / U ○ *Suigetsu* Moon Reflected on Water / I × *Uchi Shaku Taku* Inner Swamp	○ホ、人中 ×ル、胸尖 ×レ、外尺澤 ×ノ、陰囊	H ○ *Jinchu* Center of Man / U × *Munatsuki* Chest bone / Y × *Soto Shaku Taku* Outer Swamp / d × *Innoh* Secret Bag	○ニ、烏兎 ×ヌ、膻中 ○タ、稲妻 ×ヲ、甲利	B ○ *Uto* Bird Rabbit / S × *Tanchu* [Unkown] / V ○ *Inazuma* Lightning / e × *Kori* Top of the Foot

172

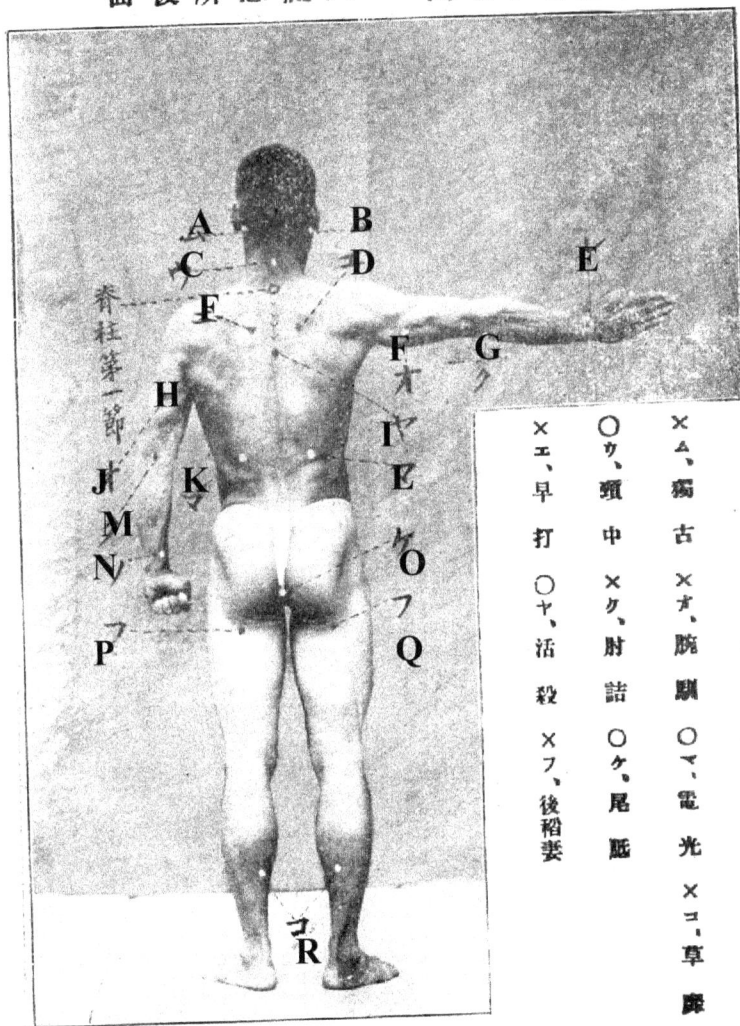

第百七十七圖　人體急所後面

×ム、獨古　×オ、腕釦　○ヤ、電光　×コ、草鹿

○ウ、頸中　×ク、肘詰　○ケ、尾骶

×エ、早打　○ヤ、活殺　×フ、後稲妻

脊柱第一節

A
B
C
D
E
F
F
G
H
I
E
J
K
M
O
N
F
P
Q
R

Translator's Note:
The readings and meanings of the points on this chart are all approxamate. There is an additonal indication of ○ or × above each point. While there is no notation saying so, this probably refers to:

○ *Sokushi* 即死 Sudden Death.

× *Sokutoh* 即倒 Sudden Incapacitation.

×エ、早打 ○ヤ、活殺 ×ア、後稲妻	**F** × *Haya Uchi* Fast Strike	○ウ、頚中 ×ク、肘詰 ○ケ、尾骶	**C** ○ *Kubichu* Center of the Neck	×ム、獨古 ×オ、腕䫏 ○マ、電光 ×コ、草鹿	**A, B** ○ *Dokko* Behind the Ear on the left and right.
	I ○ *Ka-satsu* Resussitation Point		**G** × *Hijizume* Elbow		**F** × *Udekun* Tricep
	Q × *Ushiro Inazuma* Back Lightning		**O** ○ *Bitei* Tailbone		**K** × *Denko* Lightning
					R × *Sobi* Base of the Calf

174

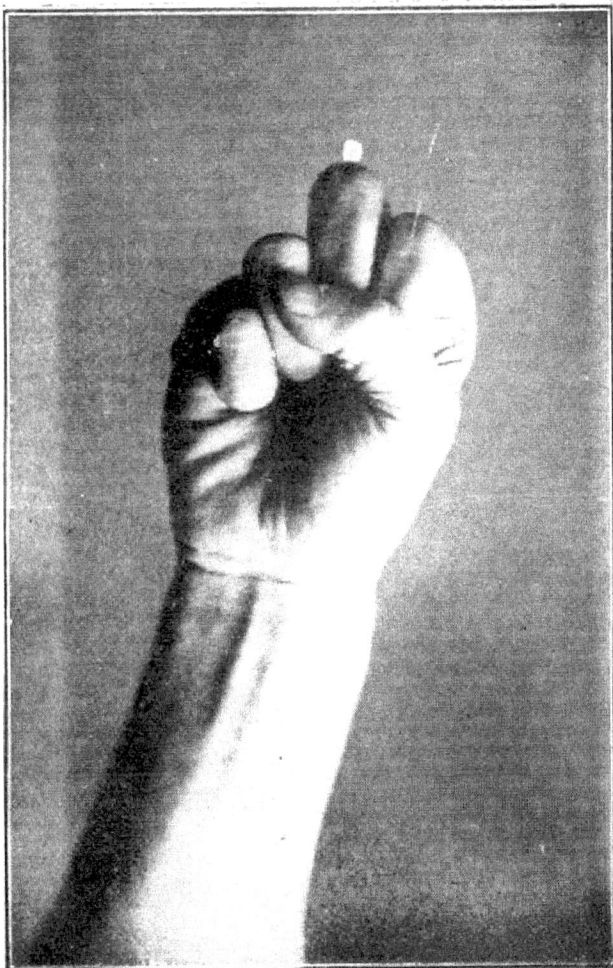

#179
Akutei Gripping Fist

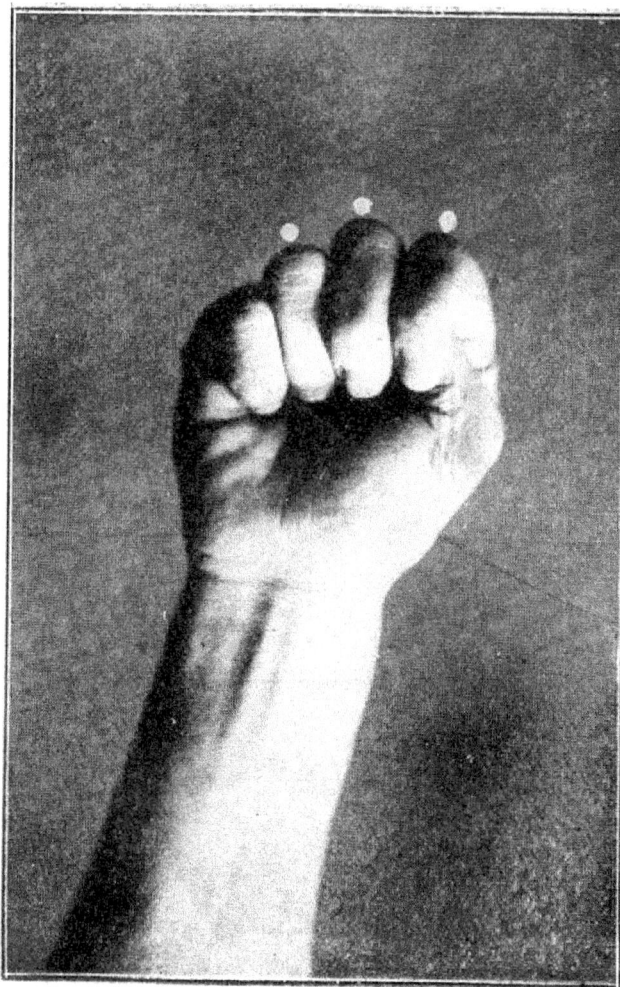

第百七十九圖　握　拳

#180
Shuto Knife Hand

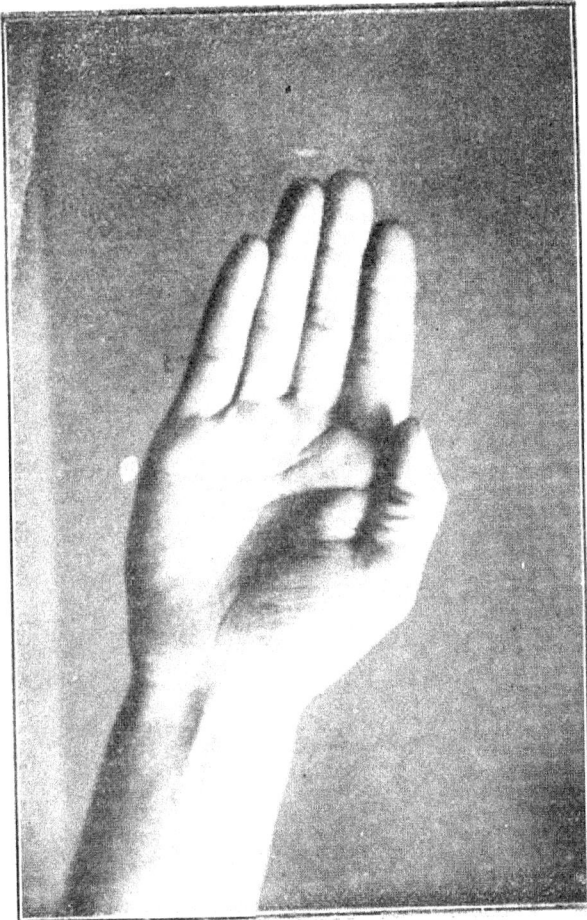

第百八十圖　手刀

#181
Sokutei Bottom of the Foot

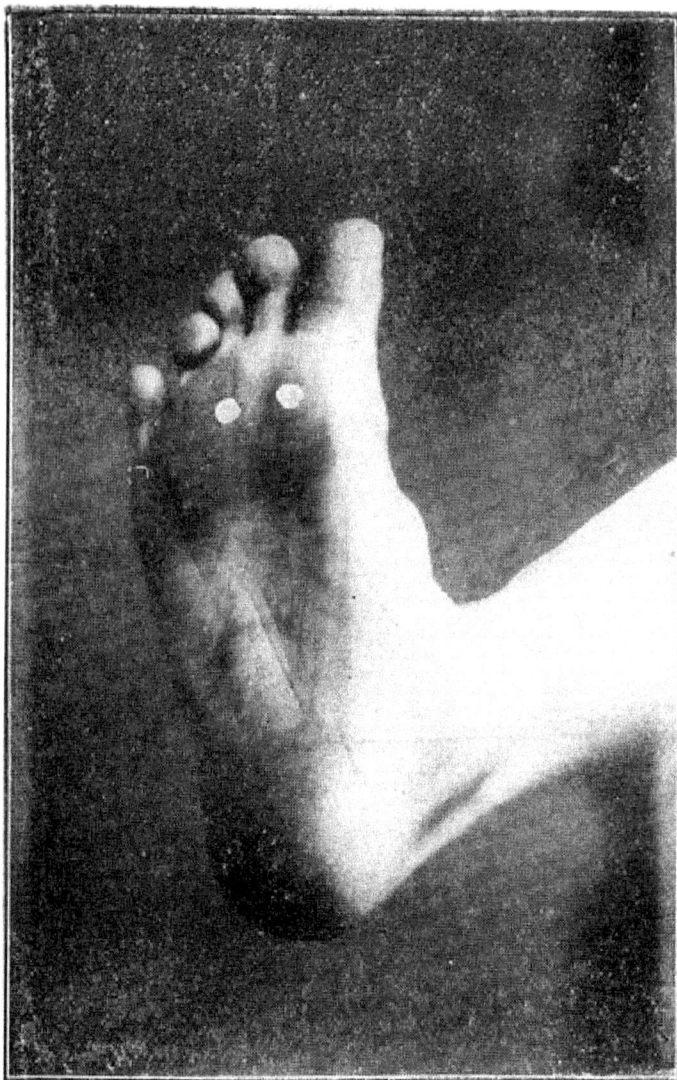

第百八十一圖 足底

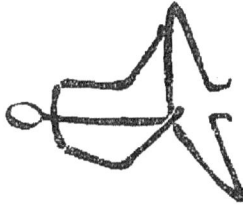

Meisei Bright Correct	*Fusui* Wind and Water	*Hasshi* Start and Stop

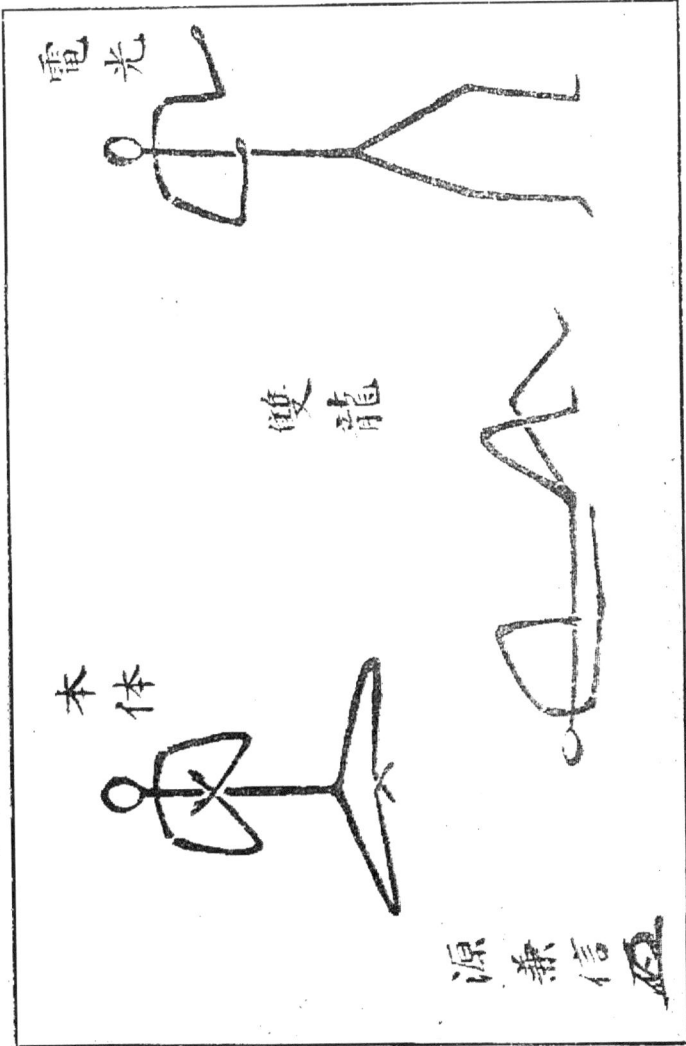

Hontai Basic Form	Soryu Double Dragon	Denko Lightning Bolt

Translator's Note:

This document is presented as a Densho, a document of transmission. It is signed Minamoto no Kanenobu 源兼信 on the bottom left. I wasn't able to find any information on him other than he was the brother of Minamoto no Kanetada 源兼忠 901-958 a Heian court official.

五、拳法基本六法

拳法は如何なる姿勢に於ても施すことの出來るものであるが、其の基本たるべき身構へ卽ち敵の精神氣力を最も容易に牽制し得る體勢は發止、風水、明正、電光、雙龍、本體の六法であることは、茲には其の

六法の解説

前に述べたところに依て略ぼ諒解し得たであらうから、體勢を解説して修行法の要概を示さう。

發止の搆

一、**發止**（第百八十二圖の一）

之は敵に向つて進退する時の構へであつて、顔を敵に向け、體は其左側を敵に向け、兩手は前に垂れ下腹の下に於て拇指を掌に交叉して四指を重ね、足の開きは常に一跡（卽ち足裏の踵より指端までの長さ）を保ち兩膝を稍屈して下腹に力を入れ、止まる

Six Fundamental Kenpo Techniques

You should be able to use Kenpo, Way of the Fist, from any position. However there are fundamental stances that can be used to counter your enemy. Depending on the disposition and attitude of your opponent you can select from the following six stances: Start and Stop, Wind and Water, Bright Correct, Lightning, Double Dragon and Main Body.

[Section omitted]

Here I will explain the meaning of each and how they should be trained.

1. Start and Stop

This is a stance you used when you are planning to either advance or retreat from an opponent in front of you. Keep your left side towards the enemy with your face looking directly at him. Your arms should hang loosely and your thumbs should be overlapped on the palms of your hands below your stomach. The four fingers of each hand should overlap as well. As always, your legs should be one Seki apart. A Seki is the distance from your heel to the tip of your toes. Your knees should be slightly bent and you should put all your power in your lower abdomen. When you stop, try to keep your right foot back. When you advance, step with your left foot first. When retreating step with your right foot first.

明正の構

風水の構

時は成るべく右足を後に踏み、進む時は左足を先きに、退く時は右足より先きにするのである。

二、風水 （第百八十二圖の二）

之は起き上がる時の構へであつて、顔を敵に向け、體は其左側を敵に向け、兩足を成るべく近づけて爪立て、兩膝は充分に開きて右膝を地に付け、右手は前に垂れて陰囊を輕く抑へ、左手は柔かき握拳となして左膝の上に乘せ、下腹に力を入れて上體を少しく左横に傾けるのである。

三、明正 （第百八十二圖の三）

之は衆敵に對する構へであつて、敵を成るべく前に受け、兩手を前後に開きて伸ばし、右足を後に踏みて左膝を少しく屈し、足の開きは三跡となし、下腹に力を入れて上體を眞直にするの

各技　當技　拳法基本六法

三四九

2. Wind and Water

This is the stance you take when you wake up. Turn the left side of your body towards your opponent as you look directly in his face. Keep your feet close together with the tips of your toes on the ground and your heels off the ground. Keep your knees comfortably apart with your right knee on the ground. Your right arm should hang loosely and should lightly cover the testicles. Your left hand should rest on your left knee and be held in a loose fist. Put power in your lower abdomen. Your upper body should be tilted slightly to your left side.

3. Bright Correct

This stance is used against multiple opponents. You should try to keep them all in front of you. Spread your arms wide in front and behind you. Plant your right foot behind you and keep your left knee slightly bent. Your feet should be about 3 Seki, foot-lengths, apart. Put power in your lower abdomen while keeping your upper body straight.

雙龍の構

電光の構

である。

四、電光 （第百八十三圖の一）

之は敵の烈しき攻撃に對する構へであつて、顔を敵に向け、體は其左側を敵に向け、右手は柔かき握拳となして輕く水月に當て、左手は握拳を敵に向けて其肘を屈し、兩膝を稍屈して足の開きを一跡半となし、下腹に力を入れて上體を眞直にするのである。

五、雙龍 （第百八十三圖の二）

之は寝たる時の構へであつて、顔を敵に向けて仰臥し、右足を充分に屈し左足を半ば屈し、右手は下方に伸べて其掌を地に付け、左手は柔かき握拳となして水月に當て、下腹に力を入れて體を少しく敵の方に捻るのである。

4. Lightning

電
光

This is a stance you take in response to a ferocious attack by an opponent. Look your opponent directly in the face, keeping the left side of your body facing him. Hold your right hand in a loose fist and place it lightly above the point called Suigetsu, Moon Reflected on Water. Your left hand is in a fist facing the opponent with your elbow slightly bent. Both knees should be bent slightly with your legs about one and a half Seki, foot-lengths, apart. Put your power in your lower abdomen and keep your upper body straight.

5. Double Dragon

This stance is used when you are sleeping. While lying on your back turn your face to your enemy. Bend your right knee sufficiently while your left knee is only half bent. Your right arm should be extended down your side, with the palm flat on the ground. Your left hand should be in a loose fist laying on top of Suigetsu, Moon Reflected on Water. Put all your power in your lower abdomen and twist your body slightly towards your enemy.

六、本體（第百八十三圖の三）

之は最も身命危き時の構へであつて、顏も體も敵に向け、兩膝を充分に開き足先を重ねて座し、兩手の甲を外にして胸に交叉し、下腹に力を入れて上體を眞直にするのである。

而して此身構の效力を確實ならしむる爲めには、其各體勢より打突、蹴の練習をなすのであつて、最初は片手に防ぐと同時に片手にて打突すること（交腕擊）を練習し、次に片手又は兩手に二つ續けて打突すること（連續擊）を練習し、次に手に打突すると見せて足にて蹴ること（交互擊）を練習し、必ず一動作毎に體勢を全く崩して其瞬間に復元との身構をなす樣にするのである。

5. Basic Form

This is the stance you should adopt when you are in extreme danger. Look directly at your opponent with your body oriented towards him. Your knees should be as wide apart as possible as you sit with the ends of your feet crossed. Your arms should be crossed on your chest with the backs of both hands facing out. While keeping your upper body straight, put power in your lower abdomen.

In order to gain the maximum benefit from all these stances it is necissary to learn how to execute every kind of strike from each stance. Therefore you must practice puching and kicking from each stance. Initally, pracice by blocking with one hand and, at the same time, striking with the other hand. This is called Kowan Geki, Alternating Arm Strike practice. Next, with either one hand or both hands train executing double strikes. This is called Renzoku Geki, Continuous Strike practice.

After that you should feint that you are going to strike with your hands, then kick. This type of training is called Kogo Geki, Alternating Strike, practice. Throughout training it is important that you do not lose your balance and you should return to the respective stance after each attack.

第百八十五圖

（其）上　同

#185 (above)
Part 2 (Continues from #184)

第百八十四圖

人工呼吸法（其一）

#184 (below)
Jinko Kokyu, Artificial Respiration.
Part 1

第百八十六圖
人工呼吸法別法

#186 (above)
Another way to perform Jinko
Kokyu Ho, Artificial
Resuscitation.

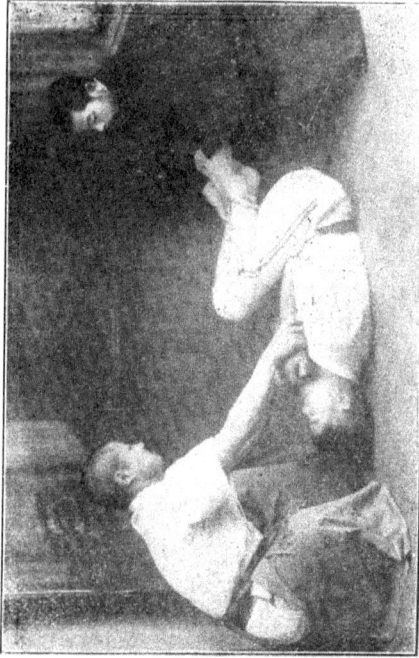

第百八十七圖
死者を起こしとするの所

#187 (below)
Raising up a *Shisha*, a person knocked
unconscious.

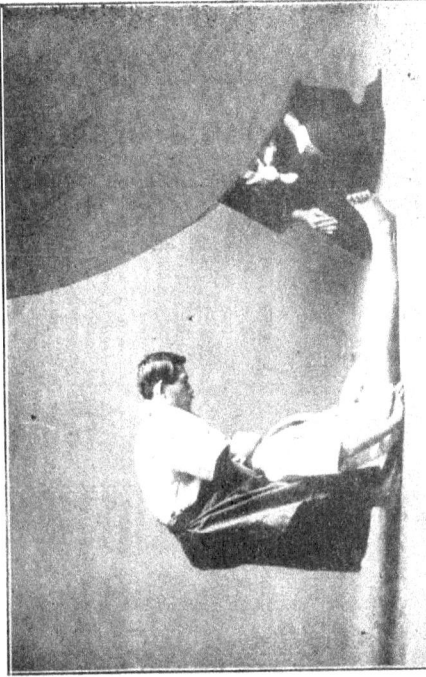

第百八十八圖

活（其一）

#188 (above)
Hai Katsu, Back Resuscitation Method.

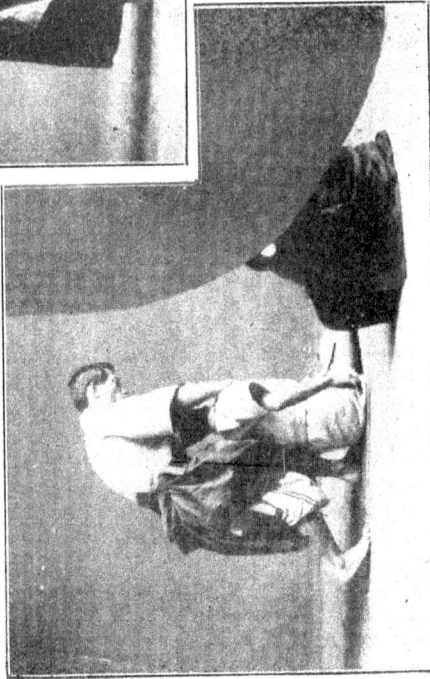

第百八十九圖

同上（其二）

#189 (below)
Another version of *Hai Katsu*, Back Resuscitation.

第百九十図
活　襟

#190 (above)
Eri Katsu, Collar Resuscitation.

第百九十一図
活　肺

#191 (below)
Hai Katsu, Lung Resuscitation.

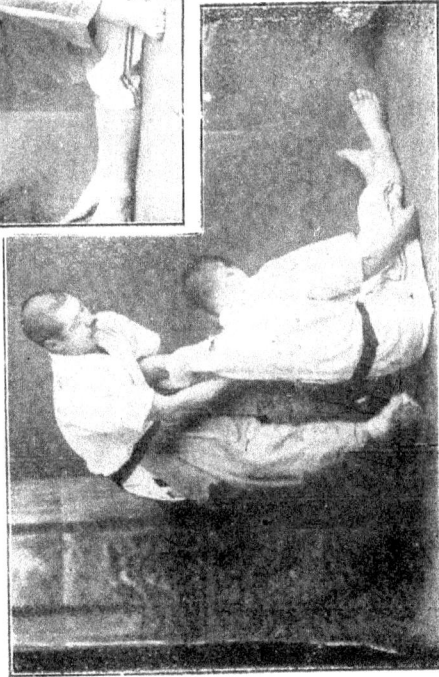

総 第百二十九図
活

#192 (above)
So Katsu, General Resuscitation.

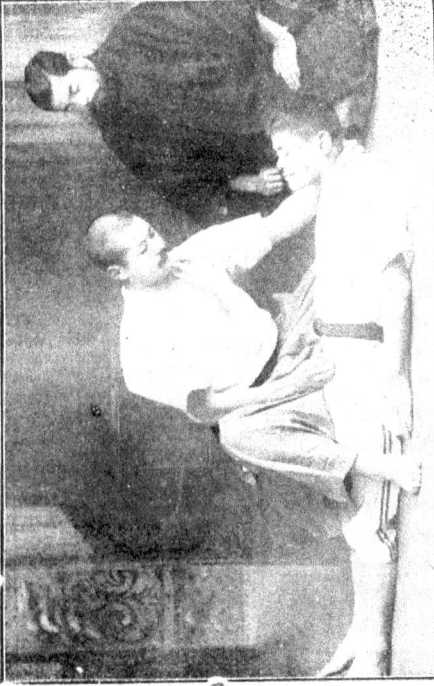

翠 第百三十図
活

#193 (below)
Koh Katsu, Testicle Resuscitation.

#194
Sui Katsu, Water Resuscitation.
Note: This is for reviving a drowned person.

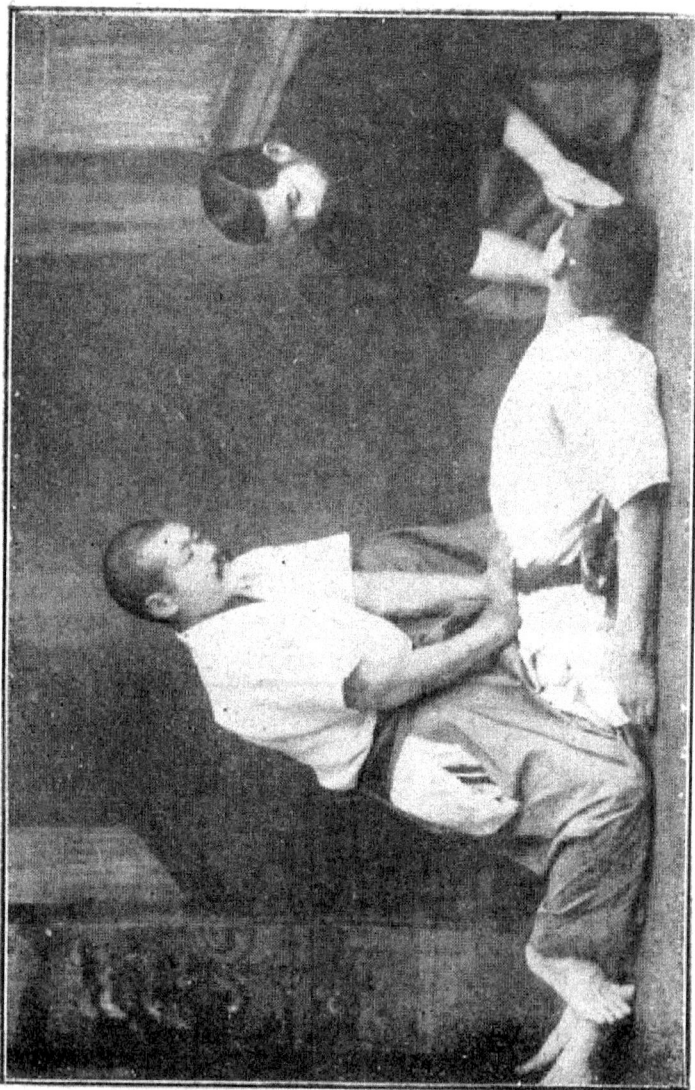

第百九十四圖　水　活

#195
Ei Katsu, Reviving a Person Who Hung Themselves.

第百九十五圖 絵

活

#196
The way you should fold your fist in this alternate way to apply
Eri Katsu, Collar Resuscitation.

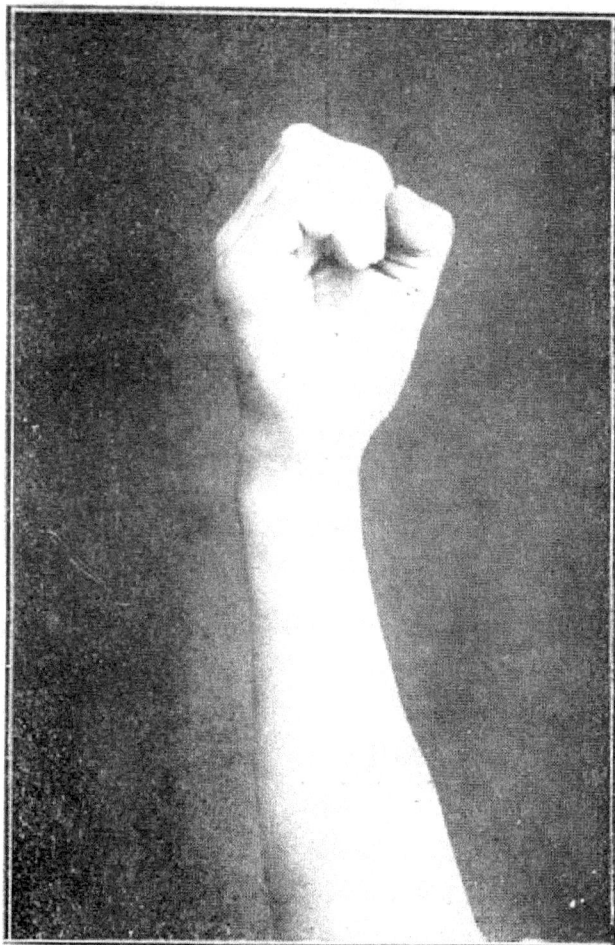

第百九十六圖　襟活別法の手

#197 (top)
The way you should shape your hand for *So Katsu*, General Resuscitation.

#198 (bottom)
Hanaji Dome, How to Stop A Nosebleed.

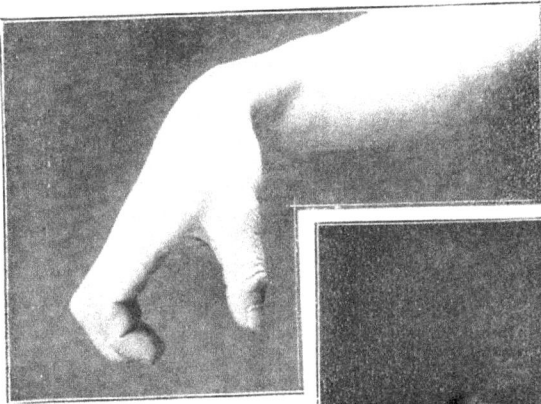

第百九十八圖

鼻　止

第百九十七圖

總　活　の　手

第百九十九圖

（其一）　法別止郎

#199
Another version of *Hanaji Dome*, How to Stop a Nosebleed. Step 1.

第二百圖

（其二）　上　同

#200 (below)
Another version of *Hanaji Dome*, How to Stop a Nosebleed. Step 2.

#200
#201

The Bones of the Body

骨の名稱

イ 前頭骨（ぜんとうこつ）
ロ 顱頂骨（ろちょうこつ）
ハ 顳顬骨（しょうじゅこつ）
ニ 後頭骨（こうとうこつ）
ホ 額骨（がくこつ）
ヘ 上顎骨（じょうがくこつ）
ト 下顎骨（かがくこつ）
チ 鎖骨（さこつ）
リ 胸骨（きょうこつ）
ヌ 肋骨（ろっこつ）
ル 脊柱（せきちゅう）
ヲ 薦骨（せんこつ）
ワ 無名骨（むめいこつ）
カ 上膊骨（じょうはくこつ）
ヨ 撓骨（たうこつ）
タ 尺骨（しゃくこつ）
レ 腕骨（わんこつ）
ソ 掌骨（しょうこつ）
ツ 指骨（しこつ）
ネ 大腿骨（だいたいこつ）
ナ 膝蓋骨（しつがいこつ）
ラ 脛骨（けいこつ）
ム 腓骨（はいこつ）
ウ 蹠骨（ふこつ）
エ 蹠骨（しょこつ）
ノ 趾骨（しこつ）
オ 肩甲骨（けんこうこつ）
ク 尾骶骨（びていこつ）

注意　第二百〇二圖は背後の肩の所を示したのである、脊柱は前面より見ゆるから別に示さないが、之を區分すれば頸の所を頸椎、肋骨のある所を胸椎、腰の所を腰椎と云ひ其下を薦骨と云ひ最下部を尾骶骨と云ふのである。

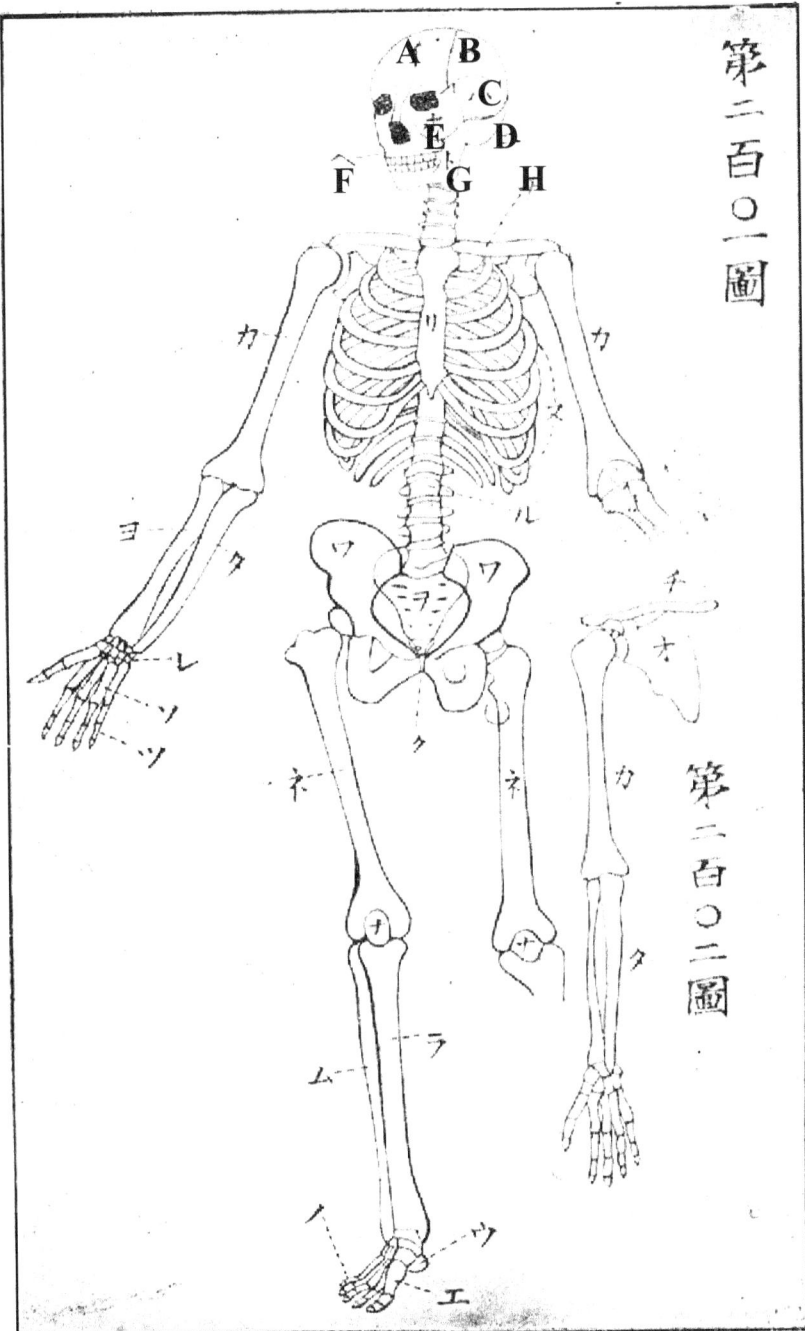

イ 前頭骨	A *Zento Kotsu* Frontal Bone of the Skull	ホ イ 顴骨	E *Kan Kotsu* Cheek bone
ロ 顱頂骨	B *Rocho Kotsu* Parietal bone	ヘ イ 上顎骨	F *Jogaku Kotsu* Upper Jaw bone
ハ 顳顬骨	C *Shoju Kotsu* Temple bone	ト 下顎骨	G *Kagaku Kotsu* Lower Jaw Bone
ニ 後頭骨	D *Goto Kotsu* Occipital bone	チ 鎖骨	H *Sakotsu* Clavicle

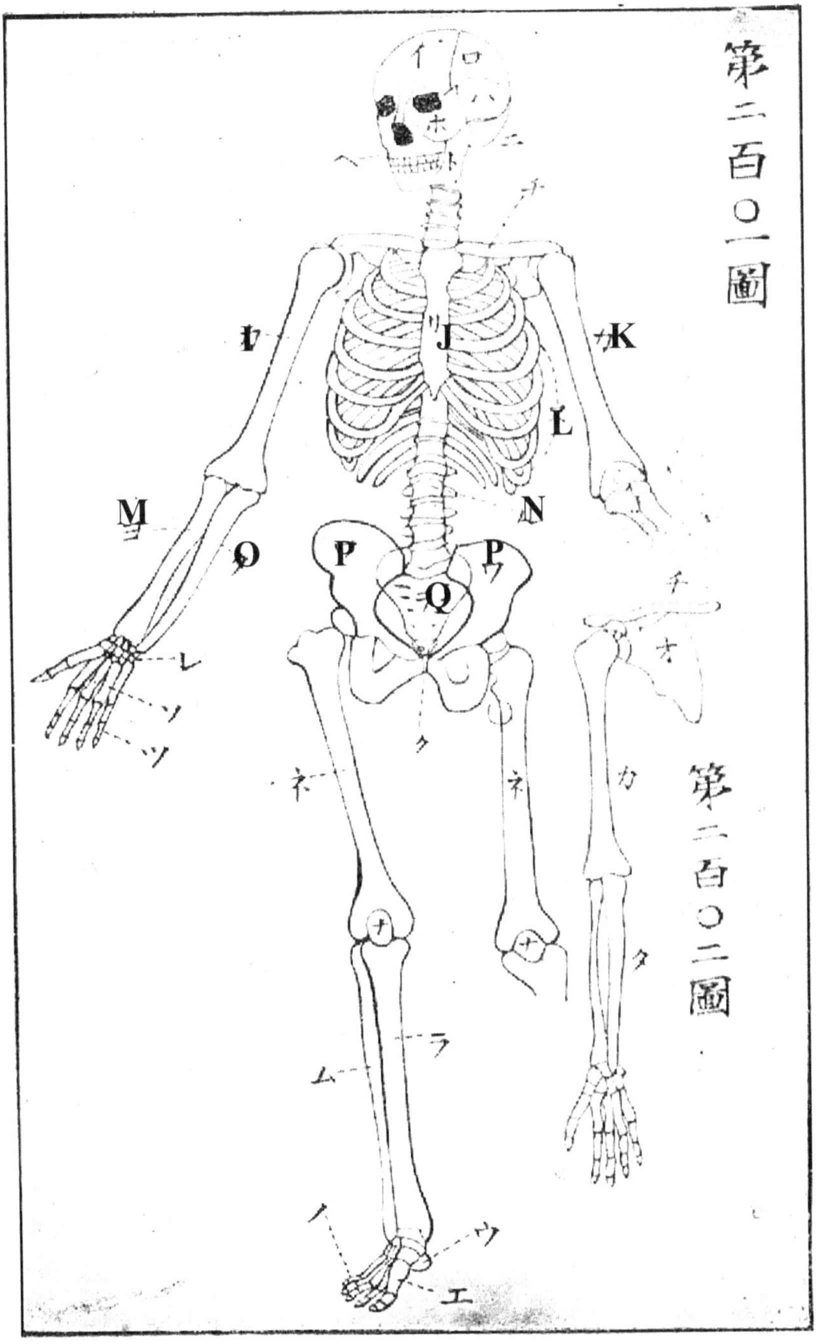

第二百〇一圖

第二百〇二圖

無名骨 ワ	P *Muna Kotsu* "Nameless bone" Pelvis	胸骨 リ	J *Kyo Kotsu* Sternum
上膊骨 カ	I *Johaku Kotsu* Humorous	肋骨 又	L *Rokkotsu* Ribs
撓骨 ヨ	M *Toh Kotsu* Radius	脊柱 ル	N *Sekichu* Spinal Column
尺骨 大腿骨 タ	O *Shaku Kotsu* Ulna	薦骨 ヲ	Q *Sen Kotsu* Sacrum

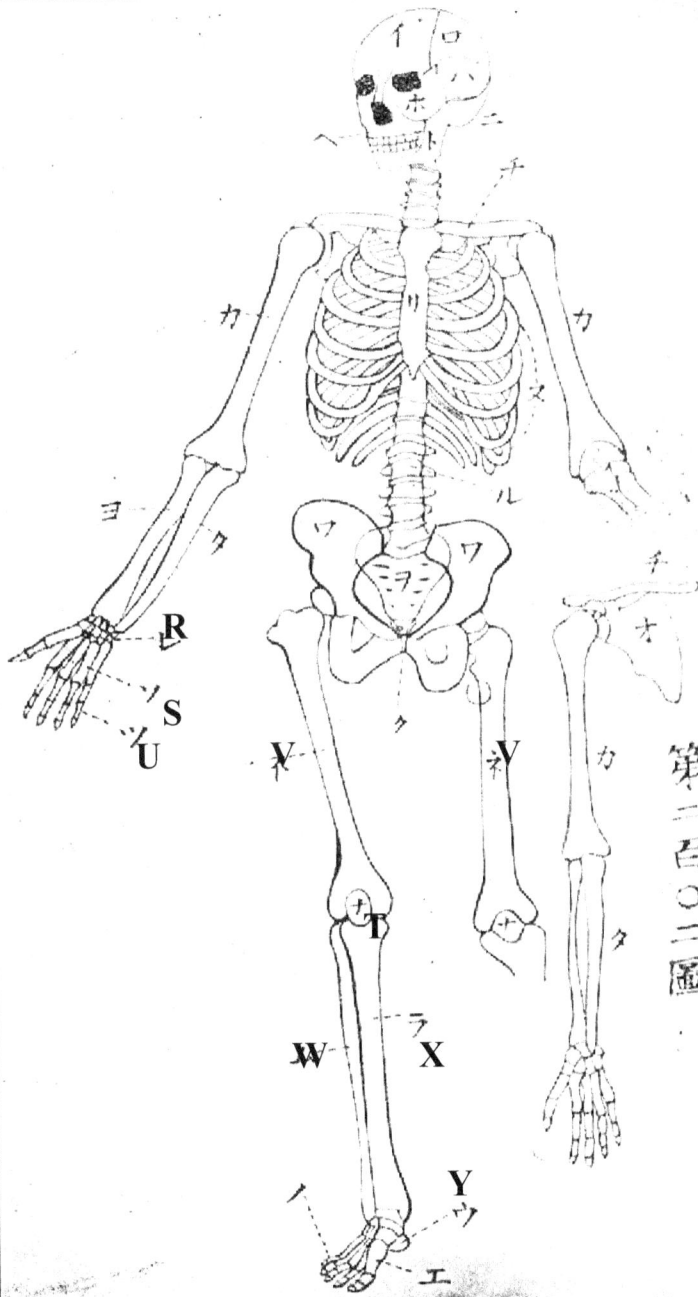

ト レ 膝 腕 しつ 蓋 がい 骨 骨 こう	**T** *Shitsugai Kotsu* Patella	レ ﾞ 宛 わん 骨 こう	**R** *Wan Kotsu* Arm Bone
ラ ソ 脛 けい 骨 こう 骨	**U** *Kei Kotsu* Tibia	リ ： 掌 しょう 骨 こう	**S** *Sho Kotsu* Wrist Bones
ム 、 腓 ひ 骨 こう 骨	**V** *Hai Kotsu* Fibula	ツ 指 し 骨 こう	**U** *Shi Kotsu* Finger Bones
ウ ・ 踵 しょう 骨 こつ	**Y** *Fu Kotsu* Heel	ネ 大 だい 腿 たい 骨 こつ	**V** *Daitai Kotsu* Femur

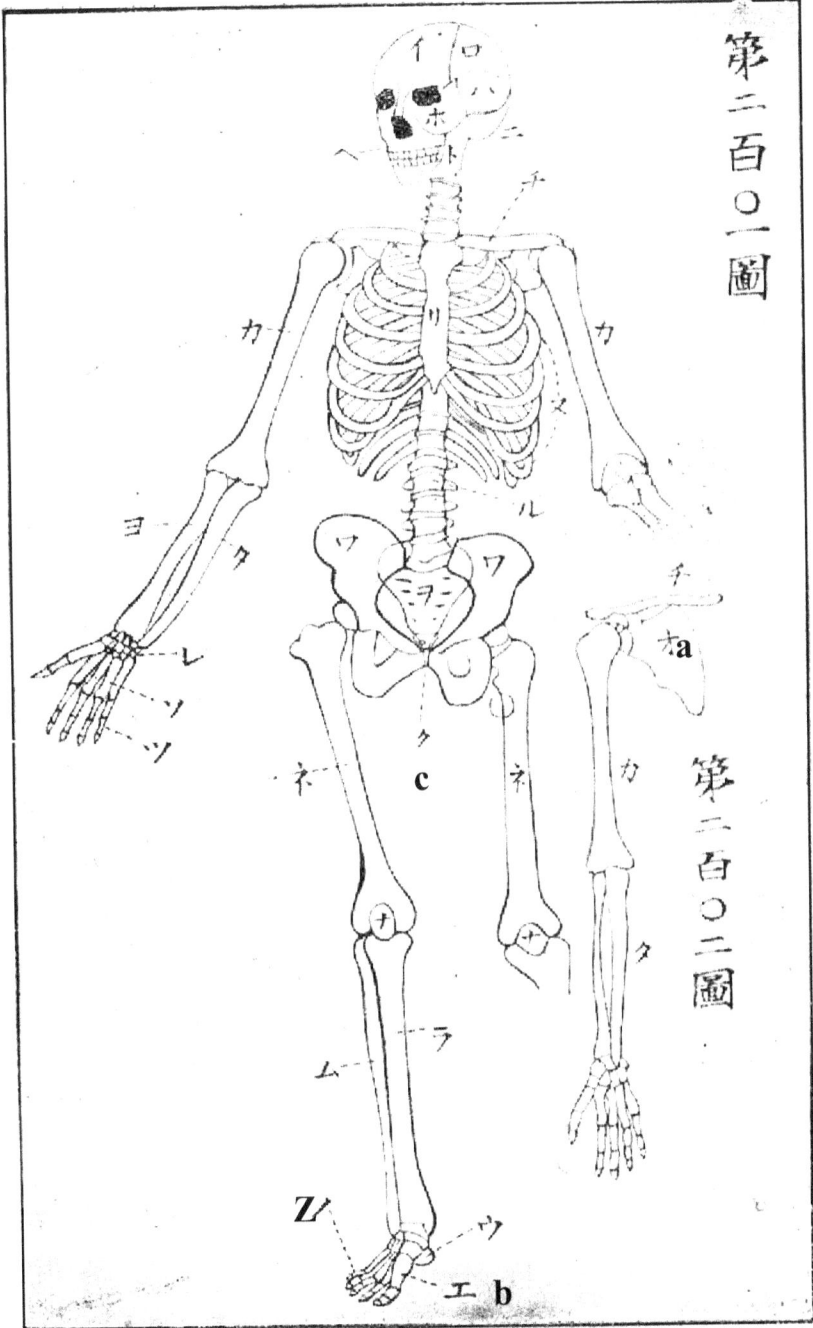

ナ 膝蓋骨 ラ 脛骨 ム 朋 尾 骨	b *Sho Kotsu* Plantar	
	Z *Shi Kotsu* Toes	 #202 This illustration shows the back of the shoulder. The spine can be seen in the first illustration so it will not be repeated.
	a *Sho Kotsu* Shoulder Blade	
	c *Bitei Kotsu* Tail Bone	

大正二年二月十七日印刷
大正二年二月二十日發行
大正二年二月廿五日再版發行

版權所有

發行所

編輯兼發行者　東京市芝區芝公園五號地
　帝國尚武會

右代表者　東京市芝區芝公園五號地
　野口正八郎

印刷者　東京市芝區三田四國町二番地
　門岡甲次郎

印刷所　東京市芝區三田四國町二番地
　三田印刷合資會社

東京芝區芝公園五號地
帝國尚武會

電話　芝〔三一〕四七九五六番
振替口座東京一九五七八番

Published by the Imperial Martial Enlightening Guild
First Printing February 12th of Taisho 2 1913
Second Printing February 25th of Taisho 2 1913

About the Authors	

Noguchi Senryuken 野口潜龍軒 (1878-1930)	Fukai Konokichi 深井子之吉 1875-?

Noguchi Sensei was born Noguchi Sei in 1878. He and his brother founded the Imperial Martial Enlightening Guild 帝國尚武 teaching Jujutsu, Kenjutsu, Suiho and Bajutsu. The school was primarily a mail order study course, which were popular in the Taisho Era. He combined six additional schools into Shin no Shindo School: Muso School, Munen School, Kito School, Yoshin Old School, Shin Kage School, and Kiraku School. This amalgam was known as Shindo Rikugo Ryu 神道六合流 New Path of Six Schools.

Fukai Sensei was born in 1875 and at the age of 16 began studying Totsuka Branch Yoshin School sword fighting. He also studied under Yamaoka Tesshu's top students. He received many awards for his bravery in the Russo Japan war and was invited to join the Imperial Martial Enlightening Guild. Though not listed specifically in the book, the techniques were developed by Fukai. The techniques in the Tiger Scroll are a combination of Totsuka Branch Yoshin School and his experiences fighting on the battlefield.

www.ingramcontent.com/pod-product-compliance
Lightning Source LLC
Chambersburg PA
CBHW071022280326
41935CB00011B/1449